FINDING YOUR LOST SELF

Your 30-Day Journey to Self-Love

for a Happy, Confident, Calm, & Less Stressed You!

DOLLY TAMPOS OKSMAN

FINDING YOUR LOST SELF
Copyright © 2023 by Dolly Tampos Oksman

ISBN:
(Paperback)   978-1959151470
(e-book)   978-1959151487

The Reading Glass Books
1-888-420-3050
www.readingglassbooks.com
production@readingglassbooks.com

Table of Contents

Special FREE Bonus Gifts for You

SELF-LOVE HABIT INVENTORY. Take this assessment so you will know where you are in your self-love habit. Please click or enter the link below to access the Self-Love Inventory.

https://www.lovehealbelieve.com/self-loveinventory

SELF-LOVE REFLECTION JOURNAL. Develop a deeper Love with your Physical, Intellectual, Emotional, and Spiritual Self. Click or enter the link below to DOWNLOAD Your FREE Reflection Journal.

https://www.lovehealbelieve.com/self-lovereflectionjournal

Thank you for purchasing this book. Part of the proceeds of this book will help fund the building of our dream center for children with disabilities in the Philippines.

DOLLY TAMPOS OKSMAN IS YOUR IDEAL PROFESSIONAL SPEAKER FOR YOUR NEXT EVENT!

All organizations that serve women, Christians, schools, and caregivers of individuals with disabilities that would like their people to live with less stress, more peace, and happiness need to hire Dolly as a keynote speaker or workshop trainer.

Love. Heal. Believe. LLC
(480)932-1487
dollyoksman@lovehealbelieve.com
www.lovehealbelieve.com

Dolly Tampos Oksman is the Creator and Author of

The Self-Love Mastery: Unlock and Love Your Authentic Self

https://www.lovehealbelieve.com/self-lovemastery

The Self-Love Initiative 30-Day Video Adventure

https://www.lovehealbelieve.com/self-loveinitiativecourse

90-Day Intensive Self-Love/Stress Reduction 1:1 Coaching. Please contact us to learn more and apply for 1:1 coaching.

https://www.lovehealbelieve.com/contact-8

From Stress to Peace 7-Day Challenge.

https://www.lovehealbelieve.com/7-daystresstopeacechallenge

Youtube Channel: Love Heal Believe Channel

Health & Wellness Blog

The Path to Bliss Podcast with Laura Sanchez-Ramirez

https://podcasters.spotify.com/pod/show/path-to-bliss

The Caring Souls Podcast

https://podcasters.spotify.com/pod/show/caringsouls

Please visit our Website, **lovehealbelieve.com**, to learn more about our products and services.

For my husband, Kimmo, my parents, Mama Coling & Papa Inting, my siblings, Jovel, Efren, Malyn & Jojo, sister-in-law, Kathy, my nephews & nieces, Jubilee Jr, Vincent James, Lawrence, Marylyn, Efren Jr., Rhea, Bea, Jhulia, Vince Albert, Lucas, and Khalista, Thank you for your love and support.

For my grandmas Nata and Juling, godfather Berto, my second mom and dad, Shirlene and Mike Lee, and Pastor Negassi Desta, for your love and for inspiring me to say "Yes!" to God's calling, thank you. I know that you are my prayer warriors now in heaven.

To God Be The GLORY Forever and Ever! Amen!

Introduction

Have you ever wondered why you always worry about how others think about you and why you need to please people and seek their approval?

Do you wonder why you feel empty? Is something missing in your life even when surrounded by people who love and care about you?

Do you wonder why love seems elusive? You try your best in your relationships, so why do you always end up with a broken heart?

More than two decades ago, I felt a deep well of emptiness. I called it an abyss because I did not know its end.

I was raised in a Catholic religious family. My mother told me that the only solution to our problems is God. So, if you have issues and struggles, you pray to God. He will listen to your prayers, especially if you are a good person. When you are good, you please God, and He will answer your prayers as a reward.

That was my belief for so long. God is only pleased with me when I'm good. He will turn His face away from me when I'm bad.

I learned the concept of "bad" and "good" from my experience with adults. For example, I was bad when the people around me were unhappy with what I did, like disobeying my parents and elders or failing at something, and received that disapproval look. I tried to create an image of a good girl at an early age to make my parents happy and, most especially, my God happy.

When I was around six or seven years old, I was sexually molested by our neighbor. Another neighbor saw what had happened. That person told me that what I was doing was terrible, and she would tell my mother. I was confused and scared. I felt terrified that my mother would know and would not be happy.

I ran to our house. I saw my mother in the kitchen. I was so scared our neighbor would show up and tell my mom what he saw. Thank God he did not show up. But, I developed a feeling of guilt.

For a while after that, I lived in the dark. I was afraid. I couldn't tell anyone what had happened because I believed what I did was terrible. I didn't want anyone to know that grievous thing I did. Eventually, I forgot the molestation incident. You might wonder how I knew if I forgot it. If you continue reading, you will learn how I uncovered this incident.

Growing up in the Philippines, at a time when virginity was highly valued, it was inculcated in me to protect my innocence. Otherwise, I would be considered unworthy of my future husband. Worst of all, my husband will return me to my family when I am no longer a virgin.

Whenever I heard this teaching about maintaining virginity, I couldn't understand why I felt so uncomfortable. Something whispered in my ears, *you better not marry. You are not worthy of your husband. No one will love you.* Also, I felt I had committed a grievous sin. I had so much guilt. I felt something was hiding within, that I was terrified would come out. I didn't know what it was. I also felt dirty, unworthy of any love. I had nightmares.

Perhaps I tried to atone for my feeling of guilt and that sexual molestation, which I thought was my fault. Maybe I tried to cover the belief that I was not worthy of love and not valuable. I became a people pleaser. I created a "Good Girl" Image. I hoped that being good would repair the damage I felt inside.

Despite my achievements and ensuing praise, and even going to church almost every day, I experienced emptiness. The void that I felt grew deeper and deeper each day. Although I continually tried harder and harder to maintain my image as a good and obedient girl, I was still unhappy. I lost myself in pleasing people. I was so stressed. From the outside, I looked ok. My parents were proud of me. I had neighbors who told me they wished their daughters were like me. On the inside, however; I hated myself and felt a silent rage towards people who said, "Inday (my nickname), you are such a kind-hearted girl." I smiled at what they said, but inside, I wanted to scream and tell them, *I am tired of being a good girl!*

I woke up one day with no sense of purpose and direction and was so lonely that I wanted to end my life. When I looked in the mirror, I saw an unfortunate girl who hated herself. Yet, deep within me, someone was crying for help. Finally, I couldn't take the anguish anymore, so I decided to end my life.

I locked myself in the bedroom. It was quiet at that time. My four siblings were not in our house. My parents were in the market. I was crying while at the same time criticizing my life and my existence. Then, when I was about to slash my wrist, I saw the Crucifix on our altar. A thought came into my head, *I love you. I died for you.* Then my mother knocked on the door. The Crucifix and the knock, brought me back from being mesmerized by the thought of ending my life. That moment brought me to my knees. I asked God to help me. I wanted to understand what was going on and why I felt the way I felt. I prayed to God to help me find the answers or let the earth open and swallow me to end my misery.

A year after that event, my friend invited me to join a youth group in the church called the Christ Youth in Action. I became so active in that organization and met amazing friends. I felt loved and accepted whenever I was with my brothers and sisters in CYA. However, when I was alone, I still felt the void. So, I thought I might serve the Lord full time and become a nun. Perhaps, becoming a nun will fill the emptiness I felt. Hence, after graduating from college, I joined a congregation. But in the convent, I felt so disturbed by the silence. I felt something scary was hunting me. I stayed in that convent for six months and then left.

More than a year after I left the convent, I met another nun. I felt comfortable talking with her and I shared with her the feeling of emptiness I carried. She told me about an unfamiliar concept which I didn't quite understand. She told me that I needed to know and love myself. I was so motivated to learn more and I decided to join their congregation.

I was in my mid-twenties at this time. Some of my friends were surprised by my decision since it wasn't too long ago that I left a convent. My good friend told me that he didn't see my calling for religious life. On the other hand, my parents were somewhat supportive. I was apprehensive, but I firmly believed that this was what I needed to do.

In the convent, the sisters introduced me to Zen Meditation, the concept of mindfulness, energy healing, self-affirmation, and the power of the mind. They gave me different tools to explore my inner world so I would come to know myself. In the process, I would understand and point out the root cause of my feeling of emptiness, the unexplainable guilt, and the fear that someone will find out. With these tools the nuns showed me, I found the answers to the whys of my unpleasant feelings. They helped me learn the secrets that took me out of my ever-present feelings of emptiness, which began by knowing and loving myself. The convent was the answer to my prayers.

I know many people experience the feeling of emptiness. So many people want to be everything for everybody to feel loved and accepted. Maybe this is you? Perhaps that is the reason why you are reading this book right now. Perhaps you are tired of being what other people want you to be. You are exhausted from living up to the standards others set for you to follow. You feel something within you wants to come out; your *authentic self.* But you are afraid that people will not accept who you are. You are worried about their criticism. You are scared that the people who love you now won't love you anymore when you show the real you. People who lack self-love may not be able to experience the fullness of their lives. They will miss the feelings of how to love and be loved unconditionally.

Many individuals are unhappy with their lives and relationships because they are not entirely free to express and receive unconditional love. They are used to the love that comes with conditions; "if you do this or do this first, then I will love you." Many people don't realize that they can experience unconditional love.

People seek love elsewhere. They think that love is out there. The sad truth is, the love you will experience out in the world is a projection of the kind of love you have for yourself. UNLESS you feel that love within that God has given you, you will not experience the fullness of love.

I want you to know that you don't have to continue to live that way. You can live a happy, meaningful life with extraordinary self-confidence, inner peace, and love by creating a habit that increases your self-knowledge and love for your authentic self.

I also want you to know that God loves and accepts you as you are. God sees beyond what other people see in you. People perceive and judge you according to your experience. But God looks at you as a wonderful creation, created in His image and likeness. There is nothing you can do for God to love you more, nor can you do anything less for him to love you less. He loves you as you. Your Creator is calling you to love yourself. He wants you to see yourself, how He sees you- God's Masterpiece. You are precious, special, and valuable.

This book will guide you on how you can love yourself. The 30-day adventures in this book will take you on a journey to self-love. In this Finding Your Lost Self, I compiled the different strategies I learned and implemented to heal myself from the sexual molestation I experienced as a child and come to love myself as I am.

Some adventures you can do right away. Some need planning, and still some need time for you to process. I encourage you to journal your experience and find time to reflect on the different reflection questions.

When you embark on this journey, please be gentle with yourself. You may encounter bumps along the way where you get frustrated or sad, but always remember it is part of the journey in life. The reward is tremendous for courageous people who hop on this adventure.

If you need further support, don't hesitate to ask for help. You can call a friend, a loved one, a therapist, or a coach like me to journey with you. Email me at dollyoksman@lovehealbelieve.com or call me at +1 480-932-1487 should you need my coaching.

We will talk more about self-love in the next chapter.

Chapter 1. Do You Love Yourself?

"If you aren't good at loving yourself, you will have a difficult time loving anyone, since you'll resent the time and energy you give another person that you aren't even giving yourself." - Barbara De Angelis.

What do you think about yourself? What do you tell yourself when you experience failure or things don't go your way? What you think and tell yourself is based on your self-concept, which is your perception of your abilities, skills, talents, personality, and other character traits.

What you think and believe about yourself will manifest in how you show up and interact with the world. For example, if you think you are beautiful and lovable, you will go out into the world with self-confidence. You will not be afraid to make mistakes, meet new people, and ask for favors because you will think of yourself as beautiful and lovable.

The same is true if you perceive yourself as inadequate and unlovable. You will exhibit these perceptions because of your insecurities and low self-esteem. When you love yourself, you have high regard for yourself.

What do you believe about yourself?

You will know if you have positive or negative perceptions about yourself by the quality of your life, and the people you are with most of the time. That is the Law of Attraction. When you think good things about yourself, that is what you project out into the universe and will therefore return to you. You feel grateful about your life. On the other hand, when you launch negativities, that is what you will receive in return. You teach people how you want them to treat you. If you want to be treated well, you must first treat yourself well.

Are you satisfied and happy with your life right now? If your answer is resounding, "NOOOOOO!" Then, I have an easy solution for you--change your self-concept. What is incredible is your self-concept isn't set in stone. It is malleable. Therefore, you can amend or reshape it. Your self-concept is open to suggestions. All you have to do is decide to change what you believe about yourself. Since your thinking, feeling, and behaving habits are affected by your perception of yourself.

It is easy to love someone you think is cool and can easily see their amazing qualities. When you perceive your *own* goodness and outstanding qualities, it is easier to love yourself as you are.

When you love yourself, you enjoy spending time with yourself in silence, taking care of yourself, and are willing to invest in your personal development. That would result in a happier, calmer, and less stressed you. Also, it would be easier for you to achieve your desired life.

Again, I want to ask you this question. Do you love yourself?

It is easy to say nice things about yourself when everything is running smoothly and going your way. However, the test of having a high regard and love for yourself is when you are experiencing difficulties and everything in your life appears imperfect.

Before proceeding to the next chapter, please reflect on the following questions and write your reflections in your journal. Then compare your answer to this question after you complete the entire adventure.

Reflect and write in your journal

　　1. What is your understanding of self-love?

_____

_____

_____

_____

2. With 1 being the lowest and 10 being the highest, how do you rate your self-love?

_____

_____

_____

_____

In the next chapter we will explore what self-love really means and debunk some common misconceptions and myths.

Chapter 2. What Self-Love Really Means

"Love yourself first, and everything else falls into line. You really have to love yourself to get anything done in this world! -Lucille Ball

What does self-love mean to you?

I spent some time exploring the concept of self-love by reading articles and listening to the conversations about this topic. I learned that there are different views and perceptions about self-love that affect how they express love for themselves.

Here are some common definitions of love and how they affect the expression of self-love.

1. **Love is a feeling**. Romantic love denotes this concept of love. It is the kind of love about which many poems and songs are written; the type of love that will take your breath away. Often, when this love strikes, you're willing to ignore everything. Sometimes you put blinders on and fail to see that the person you fall in love with is not the right one for you. When the feeling is intense, you will fail to see the "DANGER Signs" because you are in love.

However, the feeling starts to fade and leaves as time goes by. Then, you will begin to see the bad and the ugly in your partner. Finally, when trials come in your relationship, or you find someone else, you will bail out because the feeling is gone.

Though this love is common in romantic relationships, it is also present in other things, like finding a house or a job and in your journey to care for yourself.

I remember a donut chain came to our country in my younger days. I loved that place so much that I told myself I would never get tired of eating there. Guess what? After a few months, I couldn't even stand its smell. I hope you get my point.

When you think of self-love as a feeling, you will not be consistent in looking after your needs and nourishing your social, emotional, spiritual, and mental self. You will say that you love yourself and want to be better, but you won't follow through because your love depends on your feelings.

I see many people, myself included, who, after listening to an inspirational speaker, are so moved and take a step to make a change in their life. Then, at the peak of their emotions, they make decisions and promises to themselves and others, but when those heightened emotions drop, they don't follow through. Instead, they fall back into their old habits.

2. **Some people misconceive lust as love**. This type of love is based solely on physical attraction. Many people get into a relationship because there are qualities in another person that attract them. Perhaps it is their beautiful body, their hair, or how they dress. When what attracts you to the other person is gone, you will also lose that loving feeling. For example, if you are attracted to a person because of their beautiful body or perfect face, you lose attraction and your passion for that person when their physical appearance changes.

I had a friend who was wildly fascinated with a DJ on the radio. She talked about him a lot. She tried everything in her power to meet this person. At last, she did. Her attraction was gone upon seeing him. Based on his voice alone, she imagined him to appear quite different.

Have you ever wanted someone or something so much that you do everything to get it, but when you finally have it, you lose interest?

Suppose you associate self-love with lust. As a result, you will despise your body, especially if you think it does not fit the world's standard of "sexy" and "beautiful." You will think that you are unlovable. No man or woman will love you because you do not have a beautiful body and a beautiful face portrayed in magazines, TV, and other media outlets.

Many individuals struggle with their self-image and get into the habit of body shaming because they think they are not attractive enough to meet the standards advanced by social media or that they have been made to feel undesirable by family or friends.

If this is your idea of love, you may tend to express self-love by doing everything in your power to look good physically and be attractive in the eyes of other people. You will spend your money and time maintaining your youth, your beauty, and valuing yourself as a person based on your physical appearance.

3. **Love is sacrifice**. Seeing love as a sacrifice means you have to give up everything for the person you love. You have to put the people you love first before your own needs. It also means you are giving your all even if you are hurting. You may sacrifice what is fun for you and forego your dreams and desires for the sake of other people. Even if you feel unhappy, stressed, feeling empty, it is ok because you love. This kind of love is martyrdom.

To sacrifice yourself for others is a noble act. Jesus even told his disciples, "No one has greater love than this, to lay down one's life for one's friends" (John 15:13).

But to get to this level of sacrificing your life means that you, in the first place, love yourself. There is no self to offer and sacrifice if you don't love yourself.

Check your motives. What is your reason for overextending your hand?
Do you do it because of love, or do you just want to feel loved or gain attention?
Do you think you're not valuable and your needs don't matter?
Do you think it is ok for another person not to acknowledge your feelings because you deem yourself unworthy of another's consideration?

When your self-limiting beliefs drive your motives, you're not sacrificing but rather you are punishing and hurting yourself for not meeting specified expectations.

4. **Love is a commitment.** This type of love is not dependent on emotions. It is a decision to continue loving even if the feelings are not there. Love as a commitment holds onto the belief that if you maintain the relationship and continue with the loving habits, even when the feeling of love is absent, that the feeling will return.

When you are committed to someone, you will stick with that person no matter what. They may screw up a million times, and you may distance yourself for a while, but you never stop thinking about their welfare. You continue praying for them and help them in a way appropriate for you.

When you look at self-love in the same way, as a commitment, you will spend time working on yourself, whether you feel it or not.

No matter what, you will accept and love yourself as you are. You will acknowledge your limitations and weaknesses but remain committed to improving your life. You will invest your time and resources in personal growth and development.

5. **Love is selfless**. Selfless love is a higher form of love. Greeks call this *agape*-- the love that Jesus asked his disciples to have. It is unconditional love. When your love is selfless, you accept others as they are without judgment. When your love is selfless, you are full of mercy and compassion. This kind of love will compel you to commit to the people you love and provide a willingness to give yourself to them. For us Christians, Jesus showed the most remarkable example of selfless love by dying on the cross for the world's salvation.

Selfless love and sacrificial love appear the same on the outside, but the difference is within. The internal emotions one has differentiate between the two.

In one of my prayers, I asked God to let me feel what self-love is. God gave me the answer through a dream. In my dream, He showed me different faces of people who sacrificed their lives for others. I felt that they were full of LOVE.

As the dream continued, God let me experience that kind of love. While dreaming, I see myself being with the person I love, but he rejects me. However, I was filled with such love and understanding that I did not feel rejected. In my heart there was only compassion.

When I awoke, I was so filled with love. It was then that I realized that when you love selflessly, you have inner peace and joy. When you give yourself to others, doing so gives you joy. It has meaning and a purpose. There is also freedom in selfless love.

Selfless love is the opposite of sacrificial love. In sacrificial love, there is emotional pain and struggle. There is no freedom, only a burden.

How do I know this? Because I experience the difference myself. However, I never experienced the inner freedom of loving someone until I learned to love myself.

What does Self-Love mean?

According to the Brain and Behavior Research Foundation, "Self-love means having a high regard for your well-being and happiness. Self-love means taking care of your needs and not sacrificing your well-being to please others. Self-love means not settling for less than you deserve."

Self-love is accepting who you are. You take the beautiful, ugly, strengths, weaknesses, limitations, giftedness, and every aspect of you without conditions. However, even if you accept your limitations and weaknesses, you don't stay there because you love yourself. Instead, you do things to grow and develop in different areas of your life.

When the sisters told me that I needed to love myself, I was confused. For my entire life, I had believed that I needed to forget and sacrifice myself to please God. I needed "to give until it hurts." I thought that to love God is to love others and to put the interests of others first before my interest. I used to believe that God would be displeased with me if I thought about myself and cared for myself first. I was so unhappy and empty trying to follow that belief. I felt rage inside me. I hated my existence and I hated God. I wished that I wasn't born.

When I entered the convent, I was fascinated by the sisters' passion for knowing one's self. My formator (the one in charge of my formation) told me it is vital to know myself to serve others better. She said that when they send me for my mission, I may deal with people and circumstances that may trigger my past issues or contradict my inner beliefs and values. These triggers may cause emotional reactions that will affect my service to the people. It is hard for me to be proactive or objective if I don't know the source of those emotional triggers. Furthermore, my formator told me that it is also important to know my strengths and limitations because I can use them to advance our mission. Hence, the sisters showed me different strategies to better understand myself.

The process of knowing myself helps me deepen the love I have for myself. I realized that I have so much in me that needs to be celebrated. I have so much power and capabilities.

The early stage of my formation, aside from prayer and learning about our mission, was geared towards increasing my self-knowledge and accepting myself for who I am.

My formation was heavy on self-reflection or introspection. Hence, spending time in silence through prayer and meditation was embedded in our formation. In addition, the sisters, from time to time, sent me to a 7-day Zen Meditation. It was a retreat where we meditated for seven days.

In one of my meditations, I went deeper into it and uncovered the suppressed sexual molestation experience. When the memory of the sexual molestation surfaced, my body trembled. I remembered the event like a movie in my mind. I saw a frightened, confused child. Then, I felt various unpleasant emotions, pain, guilt, and fear in my body reliving the day I was molested. Then, I had a catharsis.

After the event, I went to my formator to help me. I asked her why I did not remember what had happened to me. According to my formator, that experience was so painful, my mind repressed the memories in order to cope. However, my body didn't forget. Hence, for 20 years, I carried an unexplainable feeling of guilt, unworthiness, and the fear that a secret unknown to me would emerge.

Then, I saw myself standing at the crossroads.

I had the choice to forgive, release, or hold on to the past.

I decided to enter the convent because there was something inside me that I couldn't understand. I prayed to God to show me why I felt the way I felt. Deep inside, I know that what I saw in my meditation was an answer to my prayers. God has shown me the dark side of my past so that I can bring it to light. I needed to face the shadow that hinders me from experiencing the true love, joy, and peace I long to experience.

I wanted to heal and decided to forgive and went through a healing process. During this difficult moment, I learned that when you love yourself, you want to let go of the past because you don't want bad memories or the past hurts to pull you down. You forgive because you want to be free. You forgive because you want to be healed.

I forgave those who molested me. My neighbor, who saw the incident but blamed me instead. I forgive myself for believing it was my fault.

When I started the journey of looking within myself, I began to appreciate myself more. I become more aware of the interplay of my pain, joy, trials, victories, strengths, weaknesses, and other aspects that make me unique and rare. Anything unique and rare is valuable. I am valuable! There is no other person like me. How cool is that!

Recognizing my value and worth helped me begin to love myself as me. I learned to respect and take care of myself and developed a deeper relationship with myself. I do not have to wait for others to give me their love and attention because there is so much love within me.

When I decided to put my baggage down and move forward because I love myself, I began to feel closer to my God. I became more receptive to God's presence. Now, my feeling of emptiness is gone. Instead, I experience inner peace and joy.

Self-love is a journey to your inner self so you can tap into the source of love within you. It is a prerequisite for you to love other people truly. Your ability to love others is limited when you don't love yourself. It is conditional. Therefore, you feel exhausted and stressed out by loving and angry with the people you love.

Self-love is allowing yourself to be the channel of God's love. God is love, and God, the source of love, is in you, for you are the temple of God. When you lack self-love, you block the flow of love within you.

Matthew 22:37-39 says, *"You shall love the Lord your God with all your heart, and with all your soul, and with all your mind. This is the greatest and first commandment. And a second is like it: You shall love your neighbor as yourself."*

As I continued to explore the concept of self-love, **I realized a missing piece in my interpretation of the Church's teaching.** I need to experience that love first that they instruct me to give to others.

Many Christian church leaders often emphasized loving God and loving others in their teachings. However, they don't point clearly that to love others, we need to love ourselves first because **our love for others is a manifestation of the kind of love we feel for ourselves.** Therefore, loving others begins when we love ourselves.

We cannot give what we don't have.

If we offer something we don't have, it will create a hole in us. For example, imagine you have enough money for groceries. That is all you have. Then, a friend comes to you asking for financial help. Since you are afraid of what your friend will say if you don't lend him money or perhaps you are moved with pity, you give your grocery money to your friend forcing you use your credit card instead to purchase your groceries. Now, imagine this process repeats with your other friends or family members. What will happen to you?

First, you will owe a lot of money and if you have a limited source of funds, you will end up in financial trouble, which will cause you so much financial stress. If you do not play your cards right, you might lose everything you have.

Our society often praises people who put the needs of other people first. We are labeled selfish and ungrateful if we put ourselves first over others because we are conditioned to believe that we should put ourselves last.

The sad reality is that many people who put others first without experiencing love within themselves are stressed, burned out, unhappy, and complaining. Why? It is because they are giving love without replenishing the love they give. Eventually, they run dry.

Those who receive attention, care, and affection do not always reciprocate. Instead, the givers are often taken for granted and don't even receive a simple, "thank you." So, the givers start complaining. They become emotionally drained, physically tired, mentally numb, and eventually give up on themselves and the people they love.

The truth is, if you lack love for yourself, it is hard for you to sustain your love for others. This is why Jesus commanded us to love others as we love ourselves.

When you experience this love, your compassion and understanding toward other people will expand. Your giving will no longer be a painful sacrifice but joyful because there is so much love.

It is important to remember that Self-Love comes from within you because God is in you. It is not external to yourself. It is not coming from people who offer you attention and affection that they may take back from you one day.

When you want to experience the real essence of self-love, connect within for the source of love, who is God is inside you.

When you love yourself, your world expands. You will understand others more because they have weaknesses, limitations, and struggles like you. You want people to treat you kindly when you are in your lowest moment. With more self-love, you will have compassion when others are showing their imperfect selves.

As a Christian, I believe that the ultimate expression of love is to die for others and give ourselves to others. However, we can only give ourselves if we're full of love. The overflowing love that we feel for ourselves is what we give to others. Love yourself. Take care of yourself. The truth is, by the end of the day, aside from God who loves you unconditionally, yourself is the only one you have.

What Self-Love is NOT

Let's debunk some common misconceptions and myths that will free us to take the journey to self-love.

1. **Self-love is narcissistic.** I want you to know that **you are not narcissistic when you love yourself.** Narcissism is a mental disorder. The Mayo Clinic defines Narcissistic Personality Disorder "as a mental condition in which people have an inflated sense of their own importance, a deep need for excessive attention and admiration, troubled relationships, and a lack of empathy for others."

Self-Love is appreciating and accepting yourself for who you are, not just the beautiful and the amazing in you but also the bad and the ugly. Narcissistic people dread to admit and cannot see their imperfections.

2. **Self-love is selfish.** I believe it is the other way around. You are being selfish if you don't love yourself. What happens when you are exhausted because you keep giving and giving your time, mental, physical, and emotional resources? You become stressed, easily irritated, angry, and depressed. Hence, you are not pleasant to be around anymore. Plus, you have no more strength to be with the people you love when your energy is drained. You must replenish the love you give by spending time with and caring for yourself.

Have you ever flown somewhere on a commercial airplane and listened to the flight attendants give a safety briefing? They tell the passengers that the oxygen masks will come down if needed. They ask you to put your oxygen mask on first before helping others. Why? So you will continue to live. But, what will happen if you help your child first before putting on your oxygen mask and you start to grapple for oxygen, and your young child cannot help you? Your life and the life of your child will be in trouble. Who will care for them when you die or become ill because you tried to save the needy first? If you have your mask on yourself, you can help more people who don't know how to put on their oxygen masks.

The same is true with loving yourself. You can help more people when you are healthy, happy, and at peace with your life because you care for and love yourself.

When you genuinely love yourself, it is easier to love others. I call it grace from God because you're connected to the source of love, the God within.

Love yourself. Take care of yourself.

3. Self-love and self-care are the same. Self-care is an expression of self-love; on the other hand, self-care can lead you to love yourself. Self-love centers on what we think and feel about ourselves, while self-care centers on the actions that we do for ourselves.

Some people are big on self-care, but they don't love themselves. For example, they get a regular massage, do what they love to do, and exercise, but they are hard on themselves or allow others to disrespect them continuously. Some people appear to care for their physical and mental selves to cover their low self-esteem. I once met a person who seemed to be strong and independent, but this was due to her deep internal fear that what she had in life would be lost. Her limited beliefs in herself led to this defensive posture in order to care for herself without loving herself. You can practice self-care without loving yourself, but when you have self-love, it is impossible for you not to practice self-care.

4. Self-love is Godless. When God asked us to love others, God did not say you do it alone. That is why His first commandment is to Love God above all. When you love God, you want to spend time with Him. When you spend more time with God, you can tap into the source of love, which is God. However, you can't continually draw on that source of love if you don't spend time alone with yourself and in silence to connect to the Spirit of God.

The people who lack self-love are not comfortable spending time in silence. People who do not like themselves refuse to spend time alone. Who wants to spend time with a person you don't like? No one! So, you distract yourself and create a lot of excuses to avoid spending time with yourself and avoid taking care of yourself.

In my personal experience, I did not understand God's unconditional love until I learned to love myself. I felt closer to my God when I became more comfortable with myself. I felt God's unconditional love when I accepted myself as me. Loving myself takes me to a deeper relationship with my God; when you love God, you need to love and appreciate yourself because you are God's Masterpiece.

I believe that self-love is God's gift to all of us in order for humanity to flourish. We need to take this gift. You will acknowledge and use your skills and talents to help others when you love yourself.

When you love yourself, you will experience the fullness of God's love within you.

Love conquers all and vanquishes fear. You can do the impossible with love. But, first, you must go beyond your misconceptions and blocks to love yourself.

What hinders you from loving yourself? Being a victim of sexual molestation, being compared with my friends, and being told that I was ugly created my limiting beliefs that I was not worthy hindered me from loving myself. Perhaps someone told you that if you take care of yourself first, you are selfish, making you think self-love is self-fish. As a result, you feel guilty when you give yourself attention. Thus, the guilt you feel hinders you from loving yourself.

This book will explore how we can transcend the obstructions to self-love.

In the next chapter, we will talk about your love battery. This chapter is significant to recognizing the signs you need to recharge your love battery.

Reflect and write in your journal or the space below.

1. What is your perception of self-love? How does it affect your expression of self-love?

_____

_____

_____

_____

_____

_____

_____

_____

2. Do you have any misconceptions about self-love? What are they? How did you develop them?

_____

_____

_____

_____

_____

_____

_____

_____

Chapter 3. Your Love Battery

"You yourself, as much as anybody in the entire universe, deserve your love and affection." -Buddha

My mother told me that I was different from my other siblings. I was obedient and good. I did not give them a lot of problems as a child. I smiled and secretly laughed when she said that because I remember how stressful my life had been trying to maintain the image of being good. I almost died by my own hand because of the stress.

Growing up, I tried to be well behaved in order to gain attention and love from my parents and others. I believed that I had to work hard to be loved and accepted. Still, I was unable to feel love from receiving praise. In fact, I felt used, which led me to be even harder on myself. Then, I woke up one day hating myself and silently resenting the people who told me I was good.

I felt stressed, depressed, so unlovable, worthless, and hated my life. I questioned my existence. I was mad at God and prayed that the earth would open and swallow me because I felt my life had no meaning.

I developed passive-aggressive behaviors and despised people who would tell me what to do. I felt rage inside me. I experienced a tug of war within me. Part of me wanted to be that little girl who was good and obedient. But, part of me was tired of pleasing everyone and wanted to be defiant. My Love Battery was empty.

What is a Love Battery?

The Love Battery provides a person with the source of energy to joyfully and peacefully give love and care to others. When our love batteries run low, how we interact with and serve others will be affected.

Your Love Battery is similar to the battery in your cellphone or laptop. Those devices are useless when their battery is dead and they must be regularly charged if you want to use them again. The same is true of people. You will eventually deplete your mental, physical, and emotional resources when you keep giving your energy, attention, and care to others without regularly checking your Love Battery level.

What are the indications that your Love Battery is low or empty?

1. **You are overly stressed or burned out.** When giving to people is causing you so much stress and gives you anxiety and sleepless nights, you might need to step back and charge.

2. **You find yourself complaining more often**. When you find yourself complaining that what you give is not enough. For example, you start hearing yourself say, "I tried everything for them, but they don't care, or "I did not receive even a little appreciation." When you catch yourself constantly grumbling and are unhappy when you are doing something for others, it's time for you to charge your Love Battery.

3. **You start to resent the people you help**. When you begin to feel angry with people you give your time and resources to because you don't feel appreciated or there is no reciprocation, it is a sign that your Love Battery is running low. You better be in a hurry to charge your Love Battery before you explode and your anger becomes a full rage. It is time to recharge and give yourself some love.

4. **You feel many unpleasant emotions like loneliness, depression, and emptiness.** Undesirable emotions and feelings will show up when your Love Battery is empty. Love is the fuel that drives you to get to the next level. When you have self-love, you possess an inner joy that may seem impossible to others. What can't be seen from the outside is the fire inside of you that keeps burning and allows you to feel happy to give of yourself and serve others. However, when your Love Battery is empty, there is no spark. Everything is complex and a struggle. You will feel alone and lonely, and that life has no meaning, creating a void within you.

When you start seeing those signs, your Love Battery may be running low. You need to recharge it by tapping into the source of love.

Like your cellphone or any gadget, people also need to plug in and recharge. We need to plug into our source of love; God. The good news is that you don't have to go anywhere to find God. All you have to do is to look within yourself to find the presence of God.

How will you charge your Love Battery?

Spend time with yourself in silence, prayer, meditation, introspection, and expressing gratitude. You go inward and let your spirit connect to the Spirit of God. God is the source of love. Since God is Spirit, you can connect with God through your spirit.

The Virgin Mary, mother of Jesus, sang a hymn of praise to God, known as the Magnificat. In it she said, *"My soul magnifies the Lord, and my spirit rejoices in God my savior"* (Luke 1:46-55). Magnificat shows us that our spirit can experience inner joy and pure love from God.

I know I said it is easy, but many people fear silence. It makes them feel uncomfortable because people are unsure what they will uncover about themselves in silence or are not ready to see the truth about themselves. Most of the time, who you are is revealed in silence, which is scary for many people.

Spending time alone with yourself and with your God is the best way you can fully charge your Love Battery.

When the love you feel inside you overflows, it is only then that you can serve others without expecting reciprocation. You will then stop complaining when others don't return the favor and the love you gave them. Instead, you will be filled with compassion and mercy. When you experience the overflowing love within yourself, you can accept and love yourself. You will stop judging yourself and be more compassionate. When this happens, it is easier for you to understand other people. Since you will see your reflection in them, it will be easier to let go of your judgment and be more loving and compassionate to others.

When your love battery is fully charged, you become more selective about what you allow to enter your mind and body. For example, you'll be more discerning about the types of people you allow in your life, the information you entertain in your brain, and the kind of food you allow in your body.

Your Love Battery needs to be the right kind

Using the wrong battery for a specific device will not work or damage your device. The same is true with your Love Battery.

What do I mean?

Love is magnificent, brilliant, and has different colors and interpretations. Love is highly sought after by many. People give and sacrifice their lives for it. It can make you happy or depressed. It can make you feel victorious or defeated. Often, love is misunderstood.

In the previous chapter, I mentioned the different perceptions of love and how they relate to self-love. The different perceptions of love have some truth, but some are in disguise or an imitation. Some ideas pose as love, but if you cannot transcend those feelings to a higher level of love, you may be left heartbroken at the end of the day. Imitations for love will put you on a roller coaster ride of constant emotional ups and downs.

When you want to love yourself to live a life with inner joy, peace, and meaning, you need to put on the right kind of Love Battery. The right type of Love Battery is the one that is not dependent on how you feel and what other people think or say but keeps you going to stand the test of time.

Achieving the fullness of self-love can be a challenging and lifelong process. It requires the continued discovery of how awesome you are.

Uncovering your unique, fabulous self may also mean you need to face the ghosts, monsters, and evils of your past, present, and possibly future. Unchallenged, these creatures will hinder you from really seeing your true beautiful self.

Meeting your shadows is the most complicated process in the journey. Hence, many people quit their quest for real self-love when they encounter these scary creatures.

I assure you that you can overcome these creatures and make them your friends. But, first, you must decide to commit to the process. Take one step and one habit at a time. It is hard at the beginning, but once you have the right tools and support, your journey to self-love and overcoming and making peace with these ghosts and monsters will be easier.

I did it, and I know you can do it, too.

In the following chapters, you will see the tools you can use to increase your love for yourself.

It is an adventure that will take you to the different experiences that will help your love battery be fully charged.

Reflect and write in your journal or space below.

1. What is the level of your Love Battery right now? What steps are you going to take to recharge your Love Battery?

_____

_____

_____

_____

_____

2. What challenges (i.e., shadows, ghosts from your past) have hindered you from developing a deeper love for yourself? What support do you need to help you face or overcome them?

_____

_____

_____

_____

Chapter 4. Your Self-Love Competencies

"When things change inside you, things change around you." —*Unknown*

According to the Journal of Psychology, it takes anywhere from 18 to 254 days, with the average being 66, to make a new behavior a habit. Therefore, for a new behavior to become a habit, you need to consciously practice the new behavior repeatedly until it becomes automatic.

There are four stages when you try to develop self-love habits.

The first stage is the **neophyte stage**. This means You have a lower level of self-love habits. Perhaps you don't know what self-love means and what it is all about. Then, there is no way to exert the time and effort to improve yourself and love yourself because you have no concept of it. In my case, a nun pointed out that I needed to love myself, but I didn't know what it meant or how I would develop that love. Perhaps for you, it is your friend or someone who cares about you who told you that you need to take care of and love yourself. But you don't know where to start. Awareness is vital. Hence, we become conscious of what we do that is harmful to ourselves and society at large. In this stage, you may have misconceptions about self-love, and you feel guilty when you take care of your needs before others.

The second stage is **the Nonexpert.** When you are in this stage, you have a mid-level of self-love habits. You know that you lack self-love and you have a limited understanding of it. You know some self-love habits but you don't know how to apply them in your life, so you do trial and error. Like the neophyte you have some misconceptions about self-love and from time to time you go to the extremes of expressing love for yourself.

For example, I heard of parents abandoning their children because they need to think of themselves first. Some overspend on clothes and cosmetics or take a lavish vacation that they can't afford and end up in debt.

When you know that you need to develop self-love but don't know where to begin, you can always find help. There are a plethora of resources that you can access to help you in this area. Seek, and you shall find. Enroll in our **Self-Love Mastery: Unlock and Love Your Authentic Self Program** to get started.

As part of the process during this stage, your emotional pendulum may swing to extremes. When you recognize this happening, it's time for reflection and adjustments. You will strike your balance through perseverance in your journey to self-love. Don't be discouraged, and don't give up.

The third stage is **the Competent**. You have a high level of self-love habits. In this stage, you have an increased awareness of what you are doing to develop a love for yourself. You are deliberately and consciously planning to express self-love and incorporate self-love habits into your daily activities. For example, you purposely decide not to spend too much time wallowing in pain when someone hurts or offends you. Instead, you forgive and let go. When you catch that you compare yourself with others, you transform those thoughts immediately by being grateful for what you have.

When you are in this stage, you still need to continue exploring different ways to deepen your relationship with yourself because there is still room for improvement in your expression of self-love.

The fourth stage is **the Expert**. You have a very high level of self-love habits. It is a part of you. You don't have to think about the process because it has become automatic. You act on those habits without exerting much effort. You radiate the effects of your practices to others. People ask you why you look happy, calm, at peace, or compassionate with others.

Your self-love habits will help you thrive and maintain peace and calm even during difficult times. Continue to express love for yourself. Do not stop growing and exploring more opportunities to deepen your love for yourself. Radiate your light and that love to others.

Contact me at <u>dollyoksman@lovehealbelieve.com</u> if you want more opportunities to strengthen your love for yourself.

Do you want to know what stage you are in expressing self-love? Take the Self-love Inventory at https://www.lovehealbelieve.com/self-loveinventory.

In the next chapter, various activities are provided that will help you to develop a love for yourself. Perform each activity in order to create habits and keep your Love Battery fully charged. Get ready for this transformative journey that will teach you how to love your perfectly imperfect self. Take one adventure at a time and practice what you learned on a daily basis until you create good self-love habits.

God bless you on this journey to finding your lost self.

Reflect and write in your journal or the space below

1. What stage are you in your self-love habits? Why do you think you are in that particular stage?

_____

_____

_____

_____

2. What step will you take to the next level of competency in expressing love for yourself?

_____

_____

_____

_____

Chapter 5. Commit to Find Your Lost Self

"I'm a big fan of intention. That's because I have learned first-hand the power of setting my intention on my goal and making all decisions based on that intention."
– Lewis Howes

How will you create a self-love habit that sticks?

I've learned from various mentors that for someone to form a new habit, they need to find their BIG WHY, the reason you want to change. **What is your BIG WHY?**

How to find your BIG WHY

It's been my experience that finding your WHY is easier when you reflect on how your biggest challenge affects other aspects of your life. For example, how does your current struggle jeopardize your health, relationships, finances, and other people? Then, visualize the pain that will ensue for you and those around you if you continue to struggle with the same issues. Once you've done that, visualize your life once the struggles have been resolved.

Let's use daily stress as an example. How does your stress affect your health, relationships, or job right now? Then imagine, using all of your senses (sight, touch, taste, sound, and smell), what life will be like if the stress issue is not resolved. Then visualize an alternative future where the current issue is resolved. Feel it in your heart.

When you do this exercise, you can find your BIG WHY.

Our Creator blessed us with brains that control not only the functions of our body but also protect us from dangers. A brain that doesn't want you to get hurt. Hence, always keeping an eye out for things that may harm you. I use this knowledge to trick my brain when thinking of changing a habit. Your mind doesn't know if what you experience is real or not. When using visualization, you let your body experience the pain caused by undesired habits and the happiness caused by your desired patterns. It is natural for your mind to run away from pain and go towards pleasure. The possible pain and the satisfaction you experience will be your BIG WHY.

The next step is to set your goals for completing the adventure. Formulate a plan of action that will help you achieve these goals and overcome any obstacles that come your way.

For example, if your goal is to spend 20 minutes each day over the next 30 days working on the challenges in this book, set that as your goal. Then, brainstorm how you can consistently be present each day to read the book and tackle an adventure. You also must foresee the possible obstacles that will hinder you from spending 20 minutes of your time each day. Finally, what will you do when those potential obstacles prevent you from showing up for yourself? Maybe it's your children or work demands. Ask yourself, "From what part of the day can I carve 20 minutes just for me?" If possible, stick to the same time every day. This will help you to establish a routine.

To keep you motivated to go on in creating a habit that sticks, reward yourself. Perhaps you will treat yourself after five days of being on the adventure, etc.

Reflect and write in your journal

1. What areas in your life are the most challenging for you? Write all problematic areas and identify one or two that are most challenging.

2. How are these challenges affecting your life? What will happen if your current problems are not resolved?

3. What do you really want in your life? Envision what it is that you want to feel or experience instead. Imagine the future you desire and feel it in your body.

4. How do you think developing a love for yourself will help you achieve your envisioned life?

5. What is your BIG WHY? Is it your family or a dream job? The bigger your WHY, the more you will be motivated to focus on developing self-love.

6. What self-love habits do you need to practice to achieve the life you envision?

7. What are possible obstacles that will hinder you from developing self-love habits, and how will you overcome them? Create a plan to subdue your obstacles.

On the following page, you will sign the commitment form that you will take on the journey to unlock and love your authentic self. I urge you to commit to yourself.

MY SELF-LOVE COMMITMENT

I_____ make the commitment to find time every day to deepen my relationship with myself. I will find time to care for myself and spend time with myself. I will make myself a priority from now on.

I ask the help of my God and invoke my subconscious mind to unlock the things I need to succeed in this journey.

Signature: _____ Date:_____

In the following chapter, your 30-day journey to finding your lost self will begin. Work on yourself for the next 30 days to develop a deeper self-love that will produce a happier, calmer, healthier, and more peaceful you.

Stay focused and give the next month your best effort. I know it is challenging to change your daily routine and habits. If your intention to achieve the life you want is strong enough, you will find the time.

I want to reiterate this: ask the help of God to stay motivated in order to complete this adventure, not only for yourself, but for those you love and others who you are called to serve.

Share this journey with someone you trust and ask for support or invite others to join you. **Please share or give this book to them.**

You can join 'The Self-Love Initiative Interactive 30-Day Adventure'. You can ask questions about this journey and join our group coaching.

Also, another resource we provide for you is our FREE Stress-Free Haven for Busy Women Facebook Group. You can ask questions in this group or find an accountability partner so you can continue on the journey to self-love. Or, for additional professional support or intensive one-on-one coaching to help you unlock and love your authentic self, please visit our website lovehealbelieve.com.

Remember, your intention and determination is paramount to your success.

Chapter 6. Your 30-Day Journey to Finding Your Lost Self

"I now see how owning our story and loving ourselves through that process is the bravest thing that we will ever do." -Brené Brown

In this chapter, I will guide you through creating a self-love habit. Every day for the next 30-days, you will go on an adventure to establish a deeper relationship with yourself. Go through each exercise daily. Then, pick one or two that you want to establish as a habit and do it repeatedly until you become an expert with that particular habit.

If you only do each exercise in this adventure once and only during the challenge, you can't expect it to become a habit. If you are serious about establishing a deeper relationship with yourself, you must constantly practice the activities to form a habit.

The following 30 days will be your opportunity to dive into your inner self and discover how wonderful you are. You will also learn how to treat yourself well and put yourself on the road to greater self-confidence and happiness as you better appreciate yourself.

Most of the activities on this journey can be done immediately. However, some activities need prior planning and preparation.

Developing a deeper self-love is primarily the result of your habits. The proper practices will create your desired outcomes you're looking for in your life. In 30 days, you can gain the momentum needed to make a real breakthrough in loving yourself unconditionally.

Keep an open mind. Be amazed by what you will discover about yourself. Give yourself permission to be vulnerable and have the courage to complete this adventure. Ask God for help and the grace that you will persevere in creating new self-love habits.

You can also contact me if you need further help. You visit our website lovehealbelieve.com and leave me a message.

My hope for you is that you complete this challenge and apply what you have learned to your daily life. So you can start living a life that you love to wake up to each day.

Now, grab your gear and put on your adventure clothes and let's begin the journey to self-love.

Day 1. Increase Your Self-Awareness

"Self-awareness gives you the capacity to learn from your mistakes as well as your successes. It enables you to keep growing." – Lawrence Bossidy.

How self-aware are you?

More than two decades ago, I was so unhappy, struggling with a feeling of emptiness, and not seeing the meaning of my existence. The pressure of trying to be someone I wasn't gave me so much stress. The void that I felt almost led me to death. I kept asking myself why I felt that way. Where was the feeling of emptiness coming from and what will fill that abyss within me?

One day while sitting in a philosophy class, my professor discussed the thoughts of Socrates. Two quotes in particular really impacted me: "Know Thyself" and "The unexamined life is not worth living." Hearing these words made me realize that in order to understand my feelings, I first must know myself. Around this time, I was so focused on pleasing others that I suppressed my own thoughts to the extent that I had no self-identity. I couldn't answer simple questions as to my wants without considering the wants of others.

Then I started to ask a question, easily asked, but difficult to answer, *"Who Am I?"* It took me a while to answer that question. I still look in the mirror and ask myself, "Who are you?"

My quest for self-knowledge led to my interest in understanding human behavior and psychology, which in turn led me to the convent. A nun from the Missionaries of the Assumption gave me a clear message: If I wanted to understand how I felt, I needed to know myself. She added that I also needed to love myself. I realized then that self-love is difficult if you do not first have self-awareness. Therefore, it is vital to know yourself if you want to develop a deeper love and more profound relationship with yourself. Knowing who you really are will empower you and help you reach your inner bliss. To increase your self-knowledge, you must increase your self-awareness.

Self-awareness is the first step to self-transformation. You can't change what you don't know and you will not know anything exists unless you are aware of its presence.

Self-awareness is your ability to see and understand your inner dynamics and how these affect your outer world and vice-versa. Hence, with self-awareness, you become more objective and can effectively manage your emotions, behaviors, and responses to the different circumstances you face daily. The daily habit of self-examination or reflection can help you increase your self-awareness.

Self-awareness is essential if we want to live a life of peace, joy, and harmony with ourselves and others.

Many people live a life full of misery and discontentment. They are under so much stress because they are not aligned with their values. The sad thing is they don't know that they are not aligned because they don't spend time seeing, hearing, feeling, tasting, and touching what their inner self is telling them. Our body sends us messages when something is not aligned with our internal standard: whether it be the feeling of stress, anxiety, or depression. These are signs that we need to stop and listen to realign. Unfortunately, we shoot the messenger instead. We hurt our bodies by numbing ourselves through substance abuse, workaholism, browsing social media, watching TV mindlessly, endlessly playing video games, and other forms of escape in order to bury the messages.

One of my formators in the convent told me that many people are awake physically but in a deep sleep. They eat, drink, go to work, and perform their duties and responsibilities, but they don't know what governs their actions. They think, feel, and behave in specific ways, but they are unaware of why they think, feel, and behave in certain ways. They lack self-awareness.

How can we increase our self-awareness?

I mentioned earlier that self-awareness can be achieved through self-examination and reflection. This means you must spend time alone and in silence to examine what you think, what you feel, and how you behave. Then, through self-examination, you will understand and know who you really are.

What strategies can you use for a better examination of yourself? Many vehicles can lead you to deeper self-awareness. Among these are prayer, meditation, mindfulness, and journaling.

1. **Prayer.** It is your way of communicating with your Creator—the ONE who has your blueprint. What better way of knowing who you really are other than consulting your Creator, the God who formed you in His image and likeness?

2. **Meditation.** Meditation is a way of becoming aware of your inner world. Meditation will take you on an inner journey of yourself. I learned the primary reason for my inner void during one of my meditation sessions. That horrible event from my childhood that I had buried, surfaced in my consciousness like a movie in my mind.

3. **Mindfulness.** Mindfulness is being aware of your outer world and its effect on you. When you are mindful, you increase your awareness of the present moment. Many people live in the past or future by thinking about previous events or what is yet to come. They forget to savor the present moment. They are unaware of how food affects their body or forgot to enjoy their children's smiles because their minds are elsewhere. What you have right now is all that you have. Savor it. Be present. Just Be.

4. **Journaling.** You can connect with your unconscious mind through journaling. It is also very therapeutic when you write down how you feel. Use the journaling prompts in this book or ask yourself a question and write down the answer that comes to your mind. You will be amazed at what you discover about yourself when practicing journaling. Find at least

three minutes of your time to write in your journal. You can start with one thing that catches your attention today.

5. **Thought-Watching.** Watching your thought patterns will give you a glimpse of your beliefs about yourself. It will help you uncover your limiting beliefs and the story you tell yourself that disempowers you. Your thoughts affect your feelings, your feelings affect your behavior, and the behavior you do often becomes your habits. Watch your thoughts.

Day 1 Adventure: Thought Watching Exercise

Find at least 1 to 2 minutes to be alone and watch your thoughts. Set a timer.

Take a deep breath and close your eyes. Pay attention to what you are thinking. When the timer goes off, you can gently open your eyes.

Continue to watch your thoughts throughout the day and by the end of the day, evaluate your thought patterns.

Journal your experience.

1. What are your thought patterns? Are they primarily positive or negative?

_____

_____

_____

_____

2. What thoughts are affecting your current challenge right now?

_____

_____

_____

_____

Continue to spend the next 30 days with a greater awareness of your thought patterns and how they affect your emotions, feelings, words, and behaviors.

Day 2. Affirm Yourself

"You've been criticizing yourself for years, and it hasn't worked. Try approving yourself and see what happens." -Louise L. Hay.

Do you like that person you see when you look in the mirror? As mentioned in the previous chapter, your self-concept is what you believe about yourself. Therefore, it affects what you think, how you talk to yourself, and how you behave. What do you think about yourself? How do you talk to yourself? Do you think highly of yourself, or do you loathe yourself?

According to Carl Rogers, a humanist psychologist, the self-concept has three parts; self-image, self-esteem, and ideal self.

The first part of self-concept is self-image. Your self-image is how you see yourself. It is your own perception of your various attributes and characteristics such as personality, physical traits, status, and role in society.

As a middle child who wanted attention from my parents, I tried to please them. People perceived me as a good and obedient child. This became my self-image. I hid my true feelings and calculated how I should behave in different situations to present myself as a good child, thus making others happy. Otherwise, I was no longer a good child if others were unhappy with what I did. To preserve my image, I became a people-pleaser.

Some people attach their self-image to their status and role in society. Hence, it becomes their identity. When their position in society as a CEO, the best employee, the best teacher, the best mom, or the excellent child is taken from them, they don't know who they are anymore.

The truth is how we see ourselves is not necessarily true. Some people have glorious views of themselves and others inflate their flaws and weaknesses.

What is the image you hold for yourself? Is your idea about yourself helping you become a better person or pulling you down? You need to realize that your self-image is just a perception. You are more than your self-image. The perception of others about you and your perception about yourself can change due to circumstances, like losing your job, making mistakes, or thinking you failed in something, it will not change your identity as the beloved child of God. You are still You.

The second part of self-concept is self-esteem. Your self-esteem is how you value and see your worth as a person. People with high self-esteem can accept and appreciate themselves as they are, in success and failure, in sickness and health. Our self-esteem is affected by our experiences. For example, it is shaped by how others respond to us, their approval or criticism, acceptance or rejection, which they express verbally or nonverbally.

What you believe about yourself is what you project to the world. Examine your life right now. If you are unhappy and don't like what you are experiencing, perhaps it is time to explore what you believe about yourself.

The third part of self-concept is your ideal self. The ideal self is what you wish you could be. Your self-concept is often affected when your ideal self is not aligned with your current self.

What is your ideal self?

When your ideal self is a fit woman and you are overweight, or your ideal self is in a loving relationship but you are in an abusive relationship, it affects how you think and feel about yourself. These personas will affect how you see your worth as a person and your view of yourself. Hence, it is vital to close the gap between your ideal self and current self to help improve your self-concept.

How will you change your self-concept?

You can start changing your self-concept through affirmation. Remember that self-concept is what you believe about yourself. It is not set in stone. You can change it. One of the ways you can change it is by affirming yourself.

What is self-affirmation? According to the Webster Dictionary, "Affirmation is an act of saying or showing that something is true."

Maybe you are thinking, how can I say I am good enough, beautiful, or show something true when it is not true? I AM LYING TO MYSELF when I don't see it in myself.

I know what you are thinking because the first time my formator told me about affirmation, I was uncomfortable with it because I felt I was lying to myself. It was awkward saying something you don't believe to be true. I used to think I was ugly and not good enough, and I amounted to nothing. My formator told me to look in the mirror and tell myself I am beautiful and capable of being the best I can be. I am enough.

My formator told me that if I change my limiting beliefs about myself, I will change how I feel about myself. She also reminded me that I don't lie when I tell myself that I am beautiful and perfect as I am, for I am the image and likeness of God. I just haven't seen it yet.

My formator warned me that I would not initially feel the good things I affirm to myself, but when I say it enough, I will start to believe and feel it. She also said that I would be amazed at how my new beliefs would affect how other people treat me.

The first time I did my affirmation, I felt so uncomfortable. Honestly, I laughed at it at the beginning. I told myself, who are you kidding, Dolly? Look at you; your nose is flat, and you're ugly.

When you affirm yourself, you need to attach emotions because it effectively communicates to your subconscious mind. Unfortunately, I struggled to feel good about my affirmations because I did not believe them.

One day, my formator taught us this song. "I love myself, just the way I am. There's nothing I need to change. I am always the perfect me; there's nothing to rearrange. I am beautiful and capable of being the best me I can be. I love myself just the way I am."

I loved the song. It stuck in my head! I sang the song often. I danced to it. It made me happy. The magic began when I started to sing my affirmation because it became emotionally charged. I could feel it in my body.

Soon I started to feel good about myself. I saw a new me when I looked in the mirror. I saw a loved, happy, and beautiful woman. When there was a shift in how I felt about myself, I also noticed changes in how other people treated me. I started to receive compliments from others.

From time to time, when hardship and difficulties strike me, my new beliefs and affirmations ground me.

When you struggle to affirm yourself because you don't believe what you say, pair your affirmation with your favorite song.

Here are some steps in creating a powerful, effective affirmation:

1. Affirmations should be positive and direct.
Example:
"I love myself just the way I am."
"I am beautiful and perfect as I am."

2. Connect it with your emotion.
Your affirmation will be 100X powerful when you connect it with your feelings. What better way to connect it to your emotion than attaching a melody to your affirmation--your favorite song?

For example, do you know the song "Just the Way You Are" by Bruno Mars? If you love that song, you can sing the song's chorus to yourself in the mirror or adjust the lyrics to personalize it.

3. Carry your affirmations with you.
You can keep a copy on your phone, a small notebook, or an index card. Whatever you'll consistently carry with you is fine. Consider posting them in visible places where you can see them often, like your bathroom mirror.

4. Read or sing your affirmations several times each day.
Pull out your affirmations and read them whenever you have a spare moment. Try reading them to yourself aloud when appropriate. Begin and end your day with your affirmations.

You are beautiful and perfect as you are. You can be the best you can because you're the image and likeness of God.

When you want to love yourself, you need to give yourself affirmation to reprogram those limiting beliefs that make you not love yourself.

Day 2 Adventure:

Here is your adventure today: Mirror, Mirror on the Wall Exercise.

Stand in front of the mirror. Look at yourself and find three things you love about yourself, give them affirmation and thank them. Remember to attach feelings to your affirmation.

For example, if you like your hair, say, "I love my hair. It is beautiful. It is thick, shiny, and long. Thank you, my beautiful hair, for protecting me." Or you can hug and tell yourself: I love knowing that I am loved and accepted as I am.

Journal your experience.

1. How do you feel during and after the exercise? Are there any changes in how you look at yourself?

_____

_____

_____

_____

Again, you may not feel comfortable at the beginning, but continue affirming yourself anyways. Affirmations will take time to work; you need to practice them every day. But, with repetition, you can believe in what you say.

Check out our course, <u>The Self-Love Mastery: Unlock and Love Your Authentic Self</u> to thoroughly understand how your self-concept has developed and how you could effectively change your self-concept.

Day 3. Interrupt Your Pattern

"My philosophy is to kill the monster while it's little. The best time to handle a "negative" emotion is when you first begin to feel it. It's much more difficult to interrupt an emotional pattern once it's full-blown." - Tony Robbins

Patterns are our habits or routine that we do mindlessly; meaning you do them without thinking.

Patterns are chains of behavior that lead you to your current outcome. Imagine this situation, you hit the snooze button many times before getting up leading you to wake up late. As you prepare for breakfast, your coffee maker doesn't work, your spouse or child does something that needs your attention, and now you are stressed because you are running late for work. While you're on your way to work, the traffic is terrible. Then, you start cursing at the people on the road. You are constantly looking at your watch. You are almost late for work and you have an important presentation to do. Finally, you get to work and you are officially late. Your heart is racing and pounding as you run to the conference room. Everyone is looking at you when you get in the room. Now, you feel mad at yourself and embarrassed. This chain of events causes you a lot of stress. Imagine this as your daily routine–always in a rush going to work. Always running late becomes your pattern.

What is the chain of behaviors that causes you to rush to work daily? Perhaps, you go to sleep late at night because you are browsing social media or watching the news. Then, before you go to bed, you set the alarm at a specific time to wake up, but since you went to bed late, you keep hitting the snooze button instead of getting up right away. Since you are always running late, you start your day with stress; hence, you get mad and being stressed becomes your response pattern. Our patterns are a great predictor of our day, month, year, and life.

Are you happy and satisfied with your life? Do you feel fulfilled and accomplished or do you feel frustrated, depressed, and stressed out?

Examine your patterns and become aware of those habits that cause your current outcomes. Then, do more things that make you happy and less of those that do not help you achieve your desired life.

How can you do less of your undesirable habits? Simple. Interrupt your patterns. Become aware of your patterns and consciously interrupt them. Awareness is the key to interrupting your patterns. How will you interrupt a pattern? You break away from it or disrupt it.

Think of when you were working on a project and wholly immersed in only your task. You were so focused, and then something interrupted your concentration. What happened next? That interruption snaps you out of your mental zone. You lose your focus and train of thought. When you recover from the disruption and want to continue your task, returning to what you were doing may take a moment because you are trying to figure out where you are in your project. In this state, you are open to suggestions on what you did before you were interrupted.

Pattern interruption is a strategy you can use to confuse your brain and stop it from doing what you usually do. Concurrently, you can introduce new things to your brain when you are in this state because it is open to suggestions.

I want you to reflect on your challenges right now. What behaviors or series of habits leads to the challenge? Try to interrupt the pattern. For example, what series of habits keeps you running late for work? Decide to interrupt the pattern by getting up right away when your alarm goes off.

Day 3 Adventure:

For your adventure today, you will interrupt one of your habits that causes your greatest challenge right now.

Here is what you will do.

Reflect on and answer the following in your journal or the space provided below.

1. Identify one thing that you want to improve in your life right now. Example: Your health.

_____

_____

_____

2. Find your Big Why. Why do you want to improve in that area?

_____

_____

_____

3. Identify the habits and routines you are doing that threaten your good health, for example, eating fast food or food loaded with sodium and sugar.

_____

_____

_____

4. Pick one of those habits that you will consciously interrupt today; for example, you will cook healthy food at home instead of going to a fast-food restaurant.

_____

_____

_____

Have fun interrupting undesirable patterns; this is an amazing adventure!

Day 4. Declutter Your Home Environment

"Letting go of physical clutter also declutters the mind and soul." -April Williams

Our physical environment usually mirrors our internal environment. When there is too much clutter within you, like the pain of past experiences that make you feel unhappy, and you can't let them go, it will reflect on the outside. It will show in your inability to let go of your stuff or by collecting unnecessary things.

The clutter in your environment usually manifests the chaos in your mind.

When I was on a mission trip, I met a woman who collected trash. What fascinates me is that she couldn't even let go of candy wrappers. I learned that she finds security in the stuff around her. When I was talking to her, I realized she had a lot of baggage from her past.

I want you to examine your physical living environment. Go to each room of your house. Does it look messy or is it clean and tidy? How do you feel in each of the rooms? Do you feel calm or stressed? Do you feel your body is open or constricted being there? What things do you have in those rooms that you don't need but still keep? Why are you still holding on to them?

Why do you need to declutter?

    1. Help reduce your stress. When you have too much stuff in your house you don't need, it can create unnecessary stress. For example, imagine looking for something that you cannot find right away because it is at the bottom of all of your stuff. Isn't that stressful?

    2. It allows the positive energy to flow freely. When your home environment has too much clutter, it will obstruct positive energy flow in your house. You may not know it since the energy field is not visible to most human eyes, but you feel that the air is heavy. There are blocks in your way. The environment feels tight and suffocating. Negative energy will tend to stick to your physical places. When you experience a series of unfortunate events in your life, maybe it is time to check your space. You might be obstructing the flow of positive energy in your house.

3. It will give you peace of mind. Reducing things in your area will help you clear your mind. It will minimize the chaos in your head when you see everything is organized and in the right places. Letting go of the objects you don't need is a good starting place for you to focus on the more significant issues in your life that are holding you back from achieving your desired life.

4. It will make you feel good about yourself. Imagine conquering one of the most challenging tasks, tidying your space. This endeavor is not easy. It take perseverance and a lot of courage. Letting go of objects that you have for so long because you think is valuable to you can be painful.

When you start to declutter your home and only leave what you need and love, the energy will flow freely in your space and through you. Decluttering will also allow room for anything new to come into your life. Cleaning and decluttering isn't necessarily fun, but they give you a sense of control.

How will you declutter your space?

1. Start Small. You could start organizing your desk or your cabinet, then move up to your entire walk-in closet. Then throw away what is unusable and donate the rest.

2. Keep the things that make you feel joyful. Feel the things that you have as you go through them. Which items make you feel happy at your gut level? Keep them.

3. Look at duplicates. Do you have clothes or items you unintentionally bought twice because you forgot you had purchased them before? Let go of one of them.

4. Cherish the memories, not the object. Sometimes, you tend to keep an item even if you don't need it or use it because of your memories of a particular item or its sentimental value. In this case, hold on to the memories and let go of the object.

What helps me, in this case, is to conduct a 'Letting Go Ritual.' The Letting Go Ritual helps me in my process of saying goodbye to things and people I don't need to be in my life anymore, but I am still holding on. For example, when I struggle to let go of something because of its sentimental value, this is how I do my ritual.

First, I imagine the people who gave me the object I don't need anymore. I remember the event when I receive the item. I will reminisce about what I felt at that time. Then, I thank the person and express my gratitude for the value the object they gave to me. I will also say that I kept the thing for many years because it reminds me of them. But, it is time for me to let the object go. I will tell the giver that they will be forever in my heart. Then, I say a prayer.

You can make it one of your goals to declutter your living space within 30 days. Remember, just a few minutes of decluttering each day can make a huge difference.

When you finish tidying your home environment, learn to keep things neat.

Know that you deserve to live in a clean, pleasant environment.

Day 4 Adventure:

For your adventure today, pick one room in your living space that you want to start decluttering. This room could be your bedroom, closet, kitchen, living room, garage, or wherever you are inspired to begin. Then pick one or two areas in that room that you can organize for 30 minutes or more—for example, your pantry or a kitchen drawer.

Then, in your journal or the space below, write how you feel after decluttering your space.

_____

_____

_____

_____

Happy Tidying!

Day 5. Be Ok with Imperfections

"I found in my research that the biggest reason people aren't more self-compassionate is that they are afraid they'll become self-indulgent. They believe self-criticism is what keeps them in line. Most people have gotten it wrong because our culture says being hard on yourself is the way to be." - Kristen Neff.

Do you need to be perfect?

Here is the sad news for you, perfection doesn't exist! We are human beings; we have weaknesses and limitations, so to be perfect is hard to achieve.

People who want everything perfect face frustrations most if not all the time because perfection is perception. Therefore, it depends on the eyes of the beholder. Furthermore, what you think is perfect may not be ideal for others, and what is perfect for others may not be perfect for you. Hence, our concept of perfection is subjective.

Perfectionists are frequently walking time bombs that you should watch out for as they may explode at any time.

Are you a perfectionist?

You might already know that you are a perfectionist. However, if you have doubts about it or are in denial, here are the characteristics of perfectionist people. Then, ask yourself, are you this person?

   1. Defensive. They are defensive when they receive criticism; even constructive feedback is considered a failure that will break perfectionists apart. They raise their defense mechanisms by getting mad when someone criticizes them, or they will withdraw or freeze.

   2. Quitter. They are afraid to fail because failure is imperfection, they quit easily or don't push through to achieve their goals or desired life.

3. Procrastinator. They don't want to make mistakes and they only start or finish a task if everything is perfect, making them procrastinate.

4. Emotionally Distant. They don't express their real emotion because being vulnerable is a weakness, and it will make them less perfect. They keep what they feel to themselves. They build a wall to keep the people they love and who love them from seeing their limitations.

5. Critical. They accept nothing less than perfection in their outcomes. It is not acceptable when there is even a slight imperfection.

6. Unforgiving. They are rigid and quickly spot their mistakes and criticize or sometimes punish themselves for making those mistakes. It is hard for them to forgive themselves.

7. Have low self-esteem. They seek so much approval from others. They think that they are not good enough, and people will not accept them for who they are. They try to compensate for it by creating everything perfectly to cover the imperfections they can't accept.

What are the effects of perfectionism?

Putting too much pressure on yourself to be perfect can cause anxiety, panic attacks, chronic stress, depression, burnout, and other physical and mental health problems.

Perfection is hard to achieve. You live in the shadow of how others perceive you. Your fear of being perceived as imperfect will eventually take a toll on you. It will cost your physical, spiritual, and mental health.

But aren't we called to be perfect?

Yes, we are! Those who follow a perfect God are called to be perfect. "Be perfect, therefore, as your heavenly Father is perfect." Matthew 5:48

However, it is God who is transforming us from glory to glory. To be perfect is hard to do on our own. We need God to help us. We must accept that our transformation to become perfect doesn't happen overnight, and be at peace with the truth that you are perfect as you are, and your best effort is enough.

For your health and wellness, please be ok with imperfection.

The following are some steps you can take to remove the need for perfection.

1. **Understand why you want to be perfect.** Ask yourself, "Why do you want to be perfect?" and "What beliefs do you have about perfectionism?" Journal your answers. This process can help you uncover the root cause of your perfectionism.

2. **Challenge your beliefs about perfectionism.** Your views might be inaccurate and you need to embrace a new belief system.

3. **Forgive**. Forgive yourself and understand that even if your effort is not perfect, it is the best you can do at that time.

4. **Know that imperfection is part of being human and failure is part of success.** Learn from your mistakes and failures because they will lead you to the perfection that you want in your life.

5. **Let go and let God**. Remember, it is ok to make mistakes. Put down the baggage that causes you to strive too hard for perfection and allow God to transform you from glory to glory. You don't have to do it on your own.

6. **Hire a therapist or a coach if you need help in this area and don't know where to start.** Do not be afraid to seek guidance if being a perfectionist is already affecting your well-being.

Be gentle with yourself and realize that your best effort is enough.

Day 5 Adventure:

Reflect and write in your journal or the space below. Then, take a step to let go of your need for perfection.

1. Why do you want to be perfect?

_____

_____

_____

_____

_____

2. Think of when you made a mistake, but something good came out of it; for example, you uncovered a new recipe or created something that was not what you had in mind, but it turned out to be great and wildly loved by others. How does it make you feel? This prompt will help you realize that it is ok not to be perfect.

_____

_____

_____

_____

_____

3. Write down the steps you will take to let go of your need for perfection. Then, circle one step that you will take today.

_____

_____

_____

_____

_____

Day 6. Set Your Boundaries

"The only people who get upset about you setting boundaries are the ones who were benefiting from you having none." —Unknown.

What do you do to protect your physical property from trespassers? Perhaps, you put a fence around your property with a "No Trespassing" sign. This is to let others know, "This is my property; don't come in without permission."

What will you do when someone intrudes on your property and steals something from you? You may fight the intruder, call the police or take another action to protect your physical property. In all likelihood, you will not stand by idly and watch thieves take what is rightfully yours.

If you protect your physical property, why are you not doing the same with your immaterial property? Why do you allow others to step on your emotional, mental, and spiritual boundaries? Why are you not setting limits in the first place?

Many people need approval and seek to please others so they remain unprotected and allow others to take advantage of them.

People-pleasers have an intense fear of rejection. They are afraid that people will not like them if they do not adhere to other people's demands or if they will not grant the wishes of their loved ones and friends.

Are you one of them?

I was a people pleaser myself. I understand the stress, the dilemma, and the trauma of being a people-pleaser.

When you are a people-pleaser, you say "Yes" to things you don't like and say "No" to things that matter to you in order to please others. You forego your own wants and happiness for the sake of others. You tend to suppress your feelings, don't express your thoughts, and bend your truth due to fear of what others will say and think about you.

People-pleasing behavior is an expression of self- betrayal because you are not living the life you are designed to live. As a result, you deprive yourself of reaching your full potential.

When you have no boundaries because of your desire to please people, you will experience internal conflict. This conflict springs from the disconnection of your inner self, who holds your truth that wants to come out, and your outer self that you try to project to others. This conflict will lead to a feeling of emptiness, leading to depression, unhappiness, and a life without meaning.

How will you set boundaries?

Setting boundaries is a decision you have to take. You have to decide that starting today, you will set limits and protect the boundaries you set.

Here are some tips on how to set your boundaries.

1. Know what it is that you desire in your life and your goals. When you are clear with your goals, you can say "No!" to things that will not take you to your desired life and say "Yes!" to the things that matter to you.

2. Identify the things that you value the most. What are your core values? What is important to you? Once you've identified your values, set your boundaries by eliminating those activities that are not aligned. For example, if you value your faith, family, and career, you will say "No" to things that will take you away from what you love the most.

3. Know your worth as a person. Perhaps you don't see that your existence matters. Realize that you are precious as others and what you think and feel is important. Give yourself affirmations that you are worthy.

4. Realize that it is ok to say "No." Remember, the word "No" is also a complete sentence, and you don't always need to explain the reason why you said "No."

5. Love yourself enough to protect yourself from people who want to take advantage of you. Some people just want to take and will be upset when you say, "No." It is ok. Maybe it is time for you to let go of these people.

6. Take one baby step at a time. It is hard to break this habit when you have been pleasing people all your life. Increasing your awareness of this tendency will make a big difference. Take small steps, perhaps saying "No" when someone invites you to an event you don't like.

If you are a people-pleaser and approval seeker, I have a piece of bad news for you; YOU CAN NOT PLEASE EVERYONE, no matter how hard you try. That is the sad truth.

If you don't set your boundaries, you will fall into the trap set by the people who want to take advantage of you. Let the world know what you feel, think, and need. You'll gain the respect of others and feel better about yourself. You are precious and deserve respect, but you must give it to yourself first.

Day 6 Adventure:

Reflect and write in your journal or the space below. Then, take a step to set your boundaries.

1. List down the things that you do only to please someone else in your life.

_____

_____

_____

_____

_____

_____

_____

2. From your list, pick one thing that you will say "NO" today.

_____

_____

_____

_____

3. Journal how you feel after saying "No."

_____

_____

_____

_____

_____

Day 7. Clean Up Your Schedule

"Nobody is too busy; it's just a matter of priorities." -Unknown.

How do you manage your time?

In today's world, everyone seems very busy trying to catch up with the demands of society. As a result, we are multi-tasking more than ever. At the end of the day, we end up feeling exhausted, unfulfilled, and unaccomplished because we procrastinated and left the most important tasks undone.

One evening, I talked to my mom and asked her about my sister. She said that everyone was so busy that they didn't have time to sit down and talk.

"I am busy" and "I'm stressed" seem to be the most common phrases we say now. I even catch myself saying those words. This makes sense because busyness and stress usually go hand in hand. A busy person usually is tied down by so many responsibilities, duties, and obligations that they don't have time to relax and have fun. Some people equate their success with the number of tasks they are able to check off from their to-do lists. Trying to keep up with everything that needs to be done is very stressful.

As an achiever who feels accomplished when everything on my list is marked with a check, I struggled with slowing down. Then, I realized that my busyness doesn't get me anywhere but to an exhausted mind and body.

We only have 24 hours each day and our time on earth is not limitless. I don't know when my heavenly Father will call me back home. I asked myself these questions and my way of doing things subsequently changed: "How can I make the most of the day to feel happy and content at the end? How can I better manage my time in order to enjoy fun activities? How can I make time for myself to do what I love and relax?

You may have numerous responsibilities. You are wearing different hats. You are a parent, a spouse, a member of an organization, an employee, a boss, and a caregiver of your elderly or a child with disability. Juggling all of these responsibilities is challenging and stressful. There are times that as you juggle, you drop the ball. The effect of it could be devastating because it may hurt your family.

To increase your chances of not letting a ball slip through your hands, you need to lessen the number of balls you juggle. This means being selective with the things you add to your calendar in order to maintain peace and balance.

How will you do this? Clean up your schedule by setting your priorities.

Ask yourself. What matters to you the most? What are your priorities in life?

In finding your priorities, there are two essential strategies: knowing your core values and establishing your goals in life

1. Find your core values.

Your core values are what you believe is worthwhile and worth fighting for. They are the most important to you at your core. When you follow what you value in life, you will experience harmony and balance within you. Otherwise, you will experience internal conflict. Knowing your values allows you to live an authentic life and allows you to do what's the most important.

Unfortunately, many people don't adhere to what they value. They lose touch with what is essential because they keep denying their values for fear of rejection, the need to please people, and fear of what others say.

What do you value in life? Exploring what you value in life will help you discern where you will spend your time.

How to identify your core values?

One of the best ways to uncover what you value in life is to see in your mind's eye through visualization of your future.

Go to a quiet place where you feel relaxed. Find a comfortable position, whether sitting, lying down, or even standing. Take a deep breath and then close your eyes. Now visualize your life in the future. What do you see in your life? What have you accomplish? How do you feel? Imagine when you are in your old age, see in your mind's eye what you are doing and who are the people around you? What legacy do you want to leave behind? Imagine the day of your funeral; what do you want your loved ones, friends, and colleagues to say about you?

Answering these questions will help you discover what is most important for you. For example, if you see yourself enjoying your moments with your family and grandkids in your old age, then the family is one of your core values.

You can have many values in life and you need to identify which ones are your highest priorities. You can feel confident that you're nurturing what is essential in your life. Enroll in our Self-Love Mastery Program: Unlock and Love Your Authentic Self to help uncover your life values.

2. Set Your Goals in Life.

What are your goals in life? Why do you want to achieve your goals? When you are clear with your goals and see yourself already achieving and living your dreams, it will motivate you to achieve your desired future. In addition, it will be easier for you to prioritize your activities in the process.

When you identify your values and are clear with your goals in life, you can now set your priorities. You can now create your schedule around the things that are important to you.

For example, I value my faith, health, family, work, and fun. When I create my schedule, I put them first on my daily or weekly activities. To express my faith, I include prayer and meditation in my morning routine. Then, I regularly check with my parents in the Philippines and block a time in my calendar a day with my husband and niece. I also put in my daily schedule an activity that I enjoy doing, like dancing, watching movies, or taking a hot bath.

Try it yourself. Make a list of what you value in life and your goals, then create your schedule in such a way that the list items become priorities. If you cannot manage your priorities, it is harder for you to manage your life.

Day 7 Adventure:

Reflect and write in your journal or the space below. Then, take a step to clean up your schedule.

1. Evaluate your daily, weekly, or monthly activities. List down the things you are doing that drain your energy, but you do them just because it is a routine or to please others. Then write down how much time you spend doing each activity.

_____

_____

_____

_____

_____

_____

_____

_____

2. Eliminate one or two activities on your list today that don't add to your joy. Then, replace it with something you love to do, aligned with your core values, or that will lead you closer to your goals.

_____

_____

_____

_____

_____

_____

_____

_____

Stop doing activities you don't have to do to allow you to have room for the essential things.

When you do things that align with what you value in life and what matters to you, you will be more inspired and motivated to perform those duties and responsibilities. As a result, you will feel more fulfilled and happy in life.

To help you have more time doing the things you love the most, click or enter the link below to download our free resource, **19-Time Saving Strategies for Busy Working Women.**

https://www.lovehealbelieve.com/19strategiestosavetimeworkbook

Day 8. Identify You Energy-Sucking Vampires

Have you experienced being very happy when you wake up in the morning and in an excellent mood? But, when you come to your place of work, your co-worker talks to you, and after talking to her, yo   u feel drained? Then, you notice this happens every time you talk to that coworker? That coworker might be your energy-sucking vampire.

Who and what are your energy-sucking vampires?

Energy sucking vampires are people that drain your energy. They feed on or manipulate people who are willing to listen to them. The first time I heard about these vampires was from my formator when I was in my formation to become a missionary nun. They are also called emotional vampires. Do you have people in your life that when you are around them you suddenly feel emotionally exhausted?

My formator told me that it is essential to spot these vampires. However, it is not easy to spot them, especially when they are sucking your energy slowly without your awareness. Sometimes they manipulate you to the point where you defend these vampires that suck your life away.

How to spot energy-sucking vampires? Here are some of their characteristics.

1. **Complainers**. Do you hear this, "There is always something wrong in my life." Every time they talk to you, they talk about something that ruins their life or day. Energy-sucking-vampires will always complain about someone or something and nothing seems to be right in their lives.

2. **Blamers.** The energy-sucking vampires always blame someone for what happened in their lives. Every failure, mishap, or setback is always caused by someone or something. Do you hear, "I was fired because my boss hates me?" They always point their finger at someone responsible for why they are unhappy.

3. **Needy.** The energy-sucking vampires want you to be there for them whenever they need you. The word "NO" is unacceptable to them. Guilt-tripping is their favorite game.

4. Critical. The energy-sucking vampires want you to feel insecure, so they criticize you often. They can't find what is good in you. They minimize you to make themselves look good.

5. **Exploiters.** The energy-sucking vampires thrive when they are with generous or kind hearted people. They are the energy-sucking vampires' favorite victims. They will manipulate and exploit your kindness to their advantage.

6. **Attention-grabbers.** When you share your success, the energy-sucking vampire will share an achievement that sounds higher or better than you. When you are down, and you share it with them, they will share an experience to diminish how you feel and make you think they are in lower moments than you. The attention is constantly on them.

How are you going to handle energy-sucking vampires?

Energy-sucking vampires are everywhere. You need to increase your awareness of their presence to maintain your sanity and peace of mind.

Once you spot them, the best way to approach this problem is to cut them out of your life or minimize your interaction with them. Otherwise, you will end up lifeless, unhappy, and emotionally drained.

But what if you can't cut them out entirely because they are members of your family or your co-workers, and you have no plan of finding another job?

Here are some steps you can take to handle energy-sucking vampires in your life.

1. **Set boundaries.** Learn to Say "No!" Go back to the Day 6 Adventure on how to set boundaries. Enroll in our Self-Love Mastery Program: Unlock and Love Your Authentic Self if you need more help setting boundaries.

2. **Employ planned ignoring strategy.** Planned ignoring is an Applied Behavior Analysis strategy to minimize target behavior caused by the need for attention. The energy-sucking vampires are attention seekers. To lessen their attention-seeking behavior, you deliberately ignore their behavior by not overreacting when the energy vampire comes to you and tells you of their misery. You give them a blank face or provide a short reply. You can also use your body language by closing your arms or positioning your feet away from them when they talk to you to signal that you are not available for them. Eventually, they will stop bothering you because you are no longer nourishing their emotional needs.

3. **Adjust your expectations.** The energy-sucking vampires usually lack the awareness that they are zapping your energy. They don't know that they are responsible for their outcome unless they realize that they need to be accountable for their actions. Adjust your expectations so you will not be so frustrated with them.

4. **Shield your energy field.** The battle with the energy-sucking vampire is in the energy field. Protect your energy. You can do this by visualizing a white light that covers you, or put yourself in a protective shield or bubble. Imagine that the vampires cannot penetrate your energy field.

Day 8 Adventure:

Reflect and write in your journal or the space below.

1. Who are the energy sucking-vampires in your life? Write down their names.

_____

_____

_____

_____

_____

_____

2. From your list, pick one or two of those you will minimize your contact with and write down the strategies you will use to reduce their effect on you.

_____

_____

_____

_____

_____

_____

Now, take that step to diminish the impact of the energy-sucking vampires in your life.

Day 9. Identify Your Stressors

"It's not stress that kills us, it's our reaction to it." – Hans Selye

Do you know your stress triggers? For example, can you identify why you suddenly get mad and upset when someone does or does not do something?

When you love yourself, you don't want to subject your body to constant stress and roller coaster emotions. Hence, it is vital to identify your stressors.

What are stressors?

Stressors are something or someone that triggers your stress. These could be people, events, or situations that make you feel agitated, irritated, mad, angry, upset, afraid, or depressed. Stressors are perceived external threats to which your body reacts and causes the physical reactions we know as stress which is a way for us to cope and survive.

What are your stressors?

To explain this concept, I want to share a story that led me to realize that I need to understand my stressors.

I am a special education teacher. One day, I had a new kindergarten student. When he got into my classroom, he cried. For some reason, his cry made me feel scared, sad, and angry. I felt the warm blood flow from my neck to the back of my head, then to the top. I wanted to scream at my student, "SHUT UP!" But, being aware of my body's reaction, I was able to control my response to that situation. I asked my classroom aide to take my place. I needed a break.

I went to the bathroom, wiped my face, and asked myself, "Dolly, what happened? Why did you have that intense emotional response to his cry?" I took a deep breath, composed myself, gave myself an affirmation, and said a prayer for more patience and compassion. I also prayed that I would know the reason for my reaction. Then, I went back to the classroom.

The following day the student cried again. Again, I could feel my body's reaction. But this time, it was different. I saw a vision of my grandma, beside me when I was four or five years old. I saw the neighbor come to tell her that her husband, daughter, and two of her grandchildren were killed. My grandma wailed in agony and pain. Then, I understood why I had those reactions. I associated my student's cries with death. His cries sounded similar to those of my grandmother.

Understanding the origin of my reaction helped me to process certain areas of my life in order for me to better serve my students. The next time my student cried, my reaction was less intense and eventually disappeared.

External phenomena become stressors because of the interpretation you give to events.

The meaning you attach to them is based on your beliefs, experiences, and values. When presented with something not aligned with your values and beliefs, it will threaten your comfort and status, making you feel stressed.

Your stressors will also mirror your past pain and trigger unpleasant memories that cause you to get into the fight-flight-freeze mode.

When you are interested in understanding your stressors, my **90-Day Intensive Self-love/Stress Reduction 1:1 Coaching** will help you in this area. Contact me directly to apply for this program.

Now it is your turn.

Day 9 Adventure:

Identify and become aware of your stressors. Use the *'My Personal Trigger Journal'* to track your stressors in Appendix A.

Identify the stressor that causes the greatest reaction. Try to discover the source of the stressful feelings then formulate a next step. For example, if the source is an old trauma, work on forgiving the one who caused your pain or see a therapist.

Day 10. De-stress

"To experience peace does not mean that your life is always blissful. It means that you are capable of tapping into a blissful state of mind amidst the normal chaos of a hectic life." Jill Botte Taylor

Are you under so much stress right now? If so, today is the day for you to de-stress.

Our society is fast-changing. Every day, there are discoveries, new inventions, and innovations. Our technology is incredibly advanced. Supposedly these advances will help make our lives easier and make things faster. The irony is that more people in this era experience more stress than ever trying to keep up with the demands and the need to adapt quickly to the changing technology. In addition, economic, political, and other societal problems infused by fake and opinion-driven news add to our fear and anxiety.

I felt alarmed when I heard it from my niece, who was seven years old. She told me, "I am stressed out." How could a 7-year-old who is supposed to spend more time having fun and exploring life have stress in her vocabulary? Then, she mentioned everything she had to do for school, I felt her pressure.

Many of us put more on our plates than we can chew. We demand so much from ourselves, and we try to keep up with the expectations of others and our society that we often lose time for ourselves. We struggle to keep up, which makes us experience a lot of stress.

What is stress? Maybe we need to understand this to know how to address stress from its root.

Stress is our body's reaction to strange things that make us feel uncomfortable, angry, or anxious. Our body's defense mechanism that will protect us from harm and keep us alive.

We need some stress in our lives to get through challenges in life. Stress alarms us that something is not right, not aligned with our core values and beliefs. It gives us a warning that something needs to change. We need to experience stress in order to get to another level and achieve our goals.

When we are stressed, our body releases stress hormones, Cortisol, Norepinephrine, and Adrenaline. These hormones will elevate our blood sugar, blood pressure, increase our energy, and allow us to focus on achieving our goals or ditching anything that may harm us. However, the problem is when one's body keeps releasing stress hormones. Imagine your last experience with an Adrenaline Rush. When you are stressed, scared, or overwhelmed, your body will quickly release adrenaline into your bloodstream, the "fight, flight, freeze" hormone, to cope or survive your current situation.

When I was younger, I experienced an adrenaline rush when there was a fire in our neighborhood. I used to live in a ghetto in the Philippines. Houses are so close to each other that it would be possible to burn down the entire site if there was a fire in one home. I carried a heavy item from our house to an open space outside our house and I saw my neighbor single-handedly move their television, couch, and other heavy objects.

After the fire, and by the grace of God we could go back into our house, I was unable to lift even a small item we had taken outside. I felt exhausted. I didn't want to move. I also experienced some body pain. My muscles were sore. Imagine experiencing an adrenaline rush every single day. What would happen to your body?

Stress will affect your physical, cognitive, mental, and emotional functioning. In addition, it will affect how you feel and behave. If stress is not managed correctly, it will lead to chronic illness, mental health problems, and behavior problems.

The great news is stress is your body's reaction. Therefore, you have control over it. You may have no control over the external circumstances that cause your stress. But, you have control over how you should respond to stressful situations. One of the many ways you can overcome stress is to learn how to relax, de-stress, and live in the moment. Developing an effective and healthy method of dealing with stress can help you experience inner peace and calm even during an unpleasant situation.

Here are a few healthy options for dealing with stress effectively.

1. **Pray and Meditate.** Much research shows the effectiveness of prayer and meditation in calming you down and lowering your stress level. Different studies also show that people who spend time in prayer and meditation are happier than those who don't meditate and pray.

2. **Exercise.** Move your body. Find a body movement or workout that you enjoy. It could be dancing, yoga, or going for a walk. When you exercise, your body will release the feel-good hormone. Moving your body will make you feel better. Find time in your day to move your body. According to Jim Kwik, a memory and brain coach, one of the six keys to learning faster is to exercise. He said that when you move, your brain grows. Exercise will not only decrease your feelings of stress, it can help you become smarter.

If you have limited mobility or have some injury in the part of your body, do not let it become a hindrance for you to move your body. Remember, your body is designed to move. We can train our bodies to go beyond our pain threshold. In my experience, I healed much of my body pain by moving it. However, it is always advisable to see your doctor, physical therapist, or health care provider before starting an exercise regimen.

3. **Change your Focus.** One cause of stress is when we see things are not going the way we want. It stresses us when our plan fails or when someone does not do what we expected. Instead of focusing on what went wrong, shift your attention to the things that worked and what you've learned from the experience.

4. **Learn to Let Go.** I used to live a life with so much stress. I wanted to control everything and when I experienced something that I felt I had no control over, I got frustrated, fearful, and anxious. However, things changed for me when I learned to let go of things beyond my control.

When facing a stressful situation, identify quickly what you can control and that which is beyond your control. Then, be at peace with letting go of that over which you have no control, and therefore, no jurisdiction.

I love the saying, "Let Go and Let God." It helps me remember that I have a God greater than my obstacles and problems. I offer all my struggles and concerns to God while praying for guidance for my next steps.

5. **Relax.** When you are in a position to control the things or events which cause you stress, find a solution rather than worry. Find time to relax. Do not feel guilty spending time with yourself. Please visit our website and read our blogs when you need more stress management strategies https://www.lovehealbelieve.com/dollyoksmanwellnessblogs or visit our Youtube Channel.

Day 10 Adventure:

For your adventure today, find time to de-stress and relax.

1. List down activities that you want to do that will help you de-stress.

_____

_____

_____

2. Pick one from your list that you can do today.

_____

_____

_____

3. Journal how you feel spending time to relax.

_____

_____

_____

Day 11. Forgive Others

"To forgive is to set a prisoner free and realize that prisoner was you."
-Lewis B. Smedes

Do you still hold grudges against others?

You may have times when you've been hurt or feel angry toward someone close to you. They may have said or done something that devastated you, triggered your anger, or destroyed your life. It's not easy to let go of an incident that has caused you so much pain. It is especially difficult when what they did caused you a lot of trouble, missed opportunities, and heartaches. However, forgiveness is the best gift you can give yourself. Healing comes when you learn to forgive.

Why do we need to forgive someone?

I was sexually molested when I was a child. But I did not remember the incident until I was in my 20s. However, I had mixed feelings and reactions toward men. I loved their attention, but repulsed them at the same time. I also had behaviors that I did not understand. For example, I felt ashamed of my body. I felt guilty, scared, and had an internal struggle with being unworthy. Because of that inner struggle, I was drawn to psychology and other fields that helped me understand myself.

When I joined the convent, in one of my meditation sessions, I saw the molestation incident like a movie in my mind. After that, I had a breakdown. My body was shaking. I saw a confused, scared little girl in my mind. I was crying so hard. When I calmed down, I talked to my formator and told her what I saw. Then, with an open heart, I told my formator that I needed healing.

I went through a healing process—my **breakthrough** came when I decided to forgive those who molested me. The feelings of guilt, unworthiness, and fear that no one would love me because of what had happened to me were washed away.

The forgiveness process was not easy, but I was not alone. The sisters who cared for me were there, and I prayed for the courage and the grace from God to help me. When I woke up in the morning and felt the pain of what had happened, I continued to decide to forgive until the pain was no longer there. Finally, the incident lost its grip on me. I felt free!

Do you struggle to forgive someone who hurt you? The following tips may help you to forgive.

1. **Forgiveness doesn't mean that you will forget the events that happened.** You may think that once you forgive, you forget. No, this is not the case all the time. It is hard to forget something that has a strong emotional impact on you. Forgiveness is a decision. You decide to forgive and continually make that decision, especially when you remember the pain that the events or people caused you.

2. **The pain will go away after you forgive.** There was a time when I immediately forget the pain someone caused me after forgiving them. I called it a miracle. You may have experienced this, too. However, this does not usually happen and maybe for the hurt that didn't affect your life, but when the pain is so intense, it may be hard to go away. But forgiveness should not be based on feelings. Even if you suffered great pain, try to forgive anyway. As you renew your forgiveness every time you feel the pain, you release the hurt. Though the pain may not go away instantly, its intensity will start to diminish since your focus is not on the pain anymore. Eventually, the pain will go away. You will experience inner freedom. You are free to move on and live a life of peace and with the inner joy that comes from forgiving someone.

3. **When you forgive, you do not have to restore that relationship.** You may think forgiving someone means giving them another chance to be back in your life. No, you don't have to if they will hinder you from achieving

your desired life. Sometimes you may welcome the person back in your life, but be sure to set some boundaries for yourself, to assure they will not take advantage of you. Depending on your circumstances, you can forgive someone and decide not to see them again.

4. **Unforgiveness is detrimental to your health & wellness**. Joanna Weaver, the author of "Having a Mary Spirit: Allowing God to Change Us from the Inside Out," said, "Bitterness is like drinking poison and waiting for the other person to die." When you don't forgive someone, they will become like termites in your mind and spirit, eventually destroying you. When you hold grudges, you can't sleep well at night. They will show up in your life as triggers to your stress, and you can't move forward to achieve your goals and desired life because they will hold you back. When you are angry with someone, it will give you various health problems like high blood pressure, heart problems, and even cancer.

5. **You take back your control over your life.** When you don't forgive someone, your hurt will control your life. I remember an episode on a TV sitcom, "Big Bang Theory." In that episode, Penny and Leonard had a double date with their friends Bernadette and Howard on Valentine's Day. The couple was doing fine until Penny saw her ex-boyfriend and her friend also dating. Her anger increased when her ex proposed to her friend. The scene ruined their date. Penny couldn't enjoy the company of her current boyfriend and their friends because she was too focused on her ex-boyfriend. Her grudge controlled her reactions. You lose control over yourself when you hold grudges with others. Your hurt may affect your emotions and decisions in life. You lose your freedom. When you forgive, you end that control, for you are not allowing them to affect your response, feelings, and decisions.

6. **Forgiveness may lead to reconciliation.** Reconciliation may happen when you forgive someone. The other party may realize that they hurt you and have wronged you. They may ask for your forgiveness which will amend your relationships. Thus, you can create more happy memories together.

What you focus on will expand. Hence, vengeance and resentment increase in those who refuse to forgive. The decision is yours to make. The power of forgiveness is within you. Use it for your own greater happiness.

Day 11 Adventure:

For your adventure today, forgive the person who hurt you.

To help you decide to forgive, ask yourself, "What do you want? Do you want to continue living a life feeling hurt or angry or with inner peace and joy?" When you say you want your freedom, experience inner peace and joy, and are ready to forgive, the following are the steps you will take today.

Here is what you will do.

1. **Pray.** Ask God to help you in this process of forgiveness.
2. **List the names** of people who hurt you.
3. **Acknowledge** the pain that each person on your list caused you. Imagine that they are in front of you. Tell them you are hurt for what they did to you. Express how you feel. When you finish expressing how you feel and are calm, allow them to respond to you. Listen to what they say. There might be something that they will say that will help you see the positive intention of their actions.
4. **Release** those people by telling them, "I forgive you." Imagine the pain they cause to fade away.
5. **Hug yourself when you are done.** Give yourself an affirmation for the courage to face and release those who hurt you.
6. **Write** in your journal or space below how you feel as you release and forgive the pain of your past.

_____

_____

_____

Healing begins when you forgive. Stop hurting yourself. When you don't forgive, you keep hurting yourself. When you love yourself, you want to free yourself from things that will keep you from moving to where you want to be. When you need help in forgiving others, **my 90-Day Intensive Self-love/Stress Reduction 1:1 Coaching** will help you in this area. Contact me directly to apply for this program.

Day 12. Forgive Yourself

"I think that if God forgives us, we must forgive ourselves. Otherwise, it is like setting ourselves up as a higher tribunal than God." —C.S. Lewis

Are you a human being?

If you say "YES," congratulations, you are allowed to make mistakes!

As humans, we have limitations and weaknesses; that is why from time to time, we make mistakes. One of the amazing things about us humans is that we can discern the mistakes we've made and learn from them. Please don't punish yourself for your imperfections, instead get your lessons from your mistakes.

I meet many people who can forgive others easily but can't forgive themselves. They belittle and call themselves names because of the wrong decisions they made in the past. They are hard on themselves. They keep playing with the mistakes in their heads. They are afraid to make mistakes again. This fear of making mistakes leads to perfectionism and procrastination, hindering them from moving forward to the next level of their lives.

Perhaps you are one of these people. You hate yourself because you are not what you expect yourself to be. You despise yourself because of the wrong decisions and mistakes you've made in the past.

I used to hate myself. I felt ugly and unworthy. I secretly hurt myself when I made mistakes. For example, I would slap my face, pinch my body, call myself stupid, dumb, and crazy. Things changed for me when a nun told me the concept of forgiving myself and self-love. I started increasing my awareness of how I talk to myself, especially when I make mistakes. Instead of slapping my face, I consciously changed it to hugging myself. Instead of calling myself names, I transformed those words into self-affirmation.

When you hurt yourself because of your past mistakes and are mad because you are not what everyone expects you to be or what you expect of yourself, today is the day you release yourself.

Day 12 Adventure:

For your adventure today, You will forgive and release yourself from the mistakes you've made in the past.

Reflect and write in your journal or the space below.

1. Think of a past mistake that caused significant harm to yourself and others that, until now, you still blame yourself.

_____

_____

_____

_____

2. What does it cost you to keep holding on to that past mistake? How does it affect your life?

_____

_____

_____

_____

3. Release yourself. Hug yourself and tell yourself, "I forgive you for the mistakes done in the past and for holding on to them." Reconcile with yourself. How do you feel as you release and absolve yourself from past mistakes?

_____

_____

_____

_____

_____

_____

Forgiving yourself will liberate you from your pain, and you can move forward to have inner peace and joy. Be gentle with yourself. If you continue to punish yourself, you will live a miserable, unhappy life. You will experience a void in your life. This void can only be filled when you start to forgive, accept and love yourself as you are. Learning from your mistakes will lead you to self-transformation.

Forgive yourself and move on. God has forgiven you. Why can't you?
Ask God's grace to help you as you go through the process of forgiveness.

Day 13. Purge Your Social Life

"You are the average of the five people you spend the most time with." -Jim Rohn.

How do the people you are hanging out with often make you feel?

Evaluate your social life. Look at the person you spend most of your time with every day. Then, examine your life. You might be hanging out with the wrong crowd if you don't see yourself near your ideal life, goals, and aspirations.

When I was in grade school, my teacher told us, "Birds of the same feathers flock together." Hence, she reminded us not to be friends with just anybody because friends will influence us. We must be careful if we don't want to go astray from our goals and aspirations in life.

Those words stuck in my head.

I was raised in a ghetto where drug addiction was a big problem among the youngsters because of peer pressure. I saw the detrimental effects of drug addiction and what it does to people. I tried to stay away from those companies. What helped at that time was that I had a clear vision of what I wanted to be in life. Hence, I picked friends who would help me get closer to my goals. When you love yourself, you are selective of the people you allow to come into your life, especially those you spend time with most often.

What are your goals and aspirations in life? Find those people who already have the life you want to live, hang out with them, and learn from them.

For example, when you want to be successful in your career, spend most of your time with already successful people in your field. You can also spend time with friends who encourage and support you to achieve your life's ideal.

Maybe you want to live a happy life. Still, if you surround yourself with people who speak negative stuff all the time, complainers, and downers, it is hard for you to get to the state of being happy.

When you are just starting your journey to love yourself, you must surround yourself with people who support you in this journey. Sometimes this means letting go or minimizing your interaction with people who do not help you become your best self. Unfortunately, these could be the people you love who mistreat, abuse, and treat you poorly.

Are there people in your life who take advantage of you? People in your life who make you unhappy? Do you have energy-sucking vampires in your life?

Today is your time to clean up your social life.

Cleaning up your social life may look different for you than it does for others. For example, not responding to text messages from a negative person may be a step for you to take. But, whatever it looks like, get it done. You're special and deserve to have loving people in your life.

An unknown author once said, *"Sometimes your circle decreases in size, but increases in value."* Indeed! It is better to have a few friends you can trust and who have your best interests at heart than multitudes of friends who don't really care about you..

Day 13 Adventure:

For your adventure today, is to clean up your social life.

Here are the steps that you need to take:

1. Identify what you want in your life. Write them down.
2. Make a list of everyone in your life. A spreadsheet would be perfect.
3. Examine the people on your list. How do they make you feel, order them from best to worst.
4. Start crossing out the names of the people at the bottom of your list. Pay attention to how you feel as you cross out their names. Forgive and release them. Continue crossing out the people that hold you back

from getting to where you want to be until you reach the positive and meaningful people in your life.

5. Stop or minimize your interaction with those you cross out from your list.

Day 14. Spend Time Alone with Yourself

"In the silence, we listen to ourselves. Then we ask questions of ourselves. We describe ourselves, and in the quietude, we may even hear the voice of God."
-Maya Angelou

Do you find time to be alone with yourself? Are you comfortable spending time with yourself?

Loving yourself means knowing yourself. Knowing yourself entails increasing your self-awareness which requires introspection and spending time alone with yourself.

Some people are not comfortable being alone because they feel lonely when alone. It is important to note that being alone and lonely are two different things.

Loneliness is a feeling. It is a state in which you want to be part of a social group and feel connected, but there is no one there for you. However, to be alone with yourself is a decision you make. You voluntarily do it. You withdraw yourself from your social group to be alone with yourself.

Isolating yourself to be alone is beneficial for you and your well-being. It will help you feel connected with your inner self and develop a deeper relationship with yourself. Spending time alone will boost your creativity as you explore the things you enjoy. It will boost your self-esteem as you uncover your giftedness and strengths as you come to know more about yourself. Also, spending time alone will increase your positivity as you detach yourself from people loaded with negativity and recharge your mind, body, and spirit. Further, time alone is a perfect way to reduce your stress level.

Some people, and you might be one of them, can't stand to be in their own company. They always have to be stimulated by something else. Whether on TV, the internet, the radio in the car, or a book, they can't just sit with themselves.

Have you ever wondered why you need to be on social media, constantly watching TV, listening to the radio, and doing other activities rather than spending a quiet moment with yourself?

Many people are afraid to sit alone because they do not know what they will discover or they want to escape from something and drown themselves in noise. Many fear being alone because they are scared to face their loneliness and vulnerability.

Do you fear feeling lonely? Is that the reason why you stay away from spending time alone with yourself? Do you know that you can transform loneliness into solitude? How will you transform loneliness into solitude? The following are the steps to your solitude.

1. **Change your mindset around the feeling of loneliness**. There is nothing wrong with feeling lonely. It's a mindset. Others equate being lonely with being sad. Being lonely is a feeling that needs acknowledgment. It is one of the ways your inner self communicates with you that something needs to be changed or it's calling you for something greater. It signals to your body that something needs to be restored or you need to venture into something meaningful in your life. Therefore, do not be afraid of the feeling of loneliness. Acknowledge and be grateful for it, and uncover where it wants to take you. Suppressing the feeling of loneliness will lead you to depression.

2. **Identify why you are lonely**. There are many reasons why you feel lonely. It is crucial to identify where your loneliness is coming from so you address the problems from their root cause. Maybe your loneliness is coming from the limiting beliefs you have about yourself. You can always address that by challenging those limiting beliefs. If you want to know more about this, you can join me in our Self-Love Mastery: Unlock and Love Your Authentic Self. This program will show you how you could heal your limiting beliefs.

3. **Be your best friend.** Being your best friend is vital so you can be happy being alone. You are always with yourself and might as well make you your own best friend. When I became my best friend, I seldom had dull moments. I enjoy my own company.

4. **Explore the things you love to do and do them often.** Perhaps you want to take a vacation or there is a project that you want to start. Sometimes when you're suppressing the things you love to do, your body will revolt, which will result in unpleasant emotions.

5. **Express yourself.** It is lonely when you hide your true self. It is lonely when you don't express who you are because you are afraid that people will judge you. When you cannot express yourself, you cannot attract the right people in your life. There is no greater loneliness when people surround you and adore you, but you can't be yourself. Be free to be you. Do not be afraid to express yourself. Do not be scared to be who you are. When you show your true colors, people who love your color will be attracted to you. You will attract more meaningful relationships. As Cindy Lauper's lyrics state, *"I see your true colors, and that's why I love you..."*

6. **Pray and meditate.** Prayer and meditation will help you be in touch with your inner self. It will help you know who you really are as God created you to be. Prayer and meditation will help you be connected to the higher being who created you. When you spend time in prayer and meditation, you are developing relationships with yourself and your God, who has your blueprint. These relationships will take you out of that feeling of loneliness. When you strengthen your relationship with yourself and your God, spending time alone will be easier. You will feel more comfortable. You will experience the real sense of the phrase, *"Alone but not lonely."*

What are the things you can do when you are alone with yourself? **Here are some ideas you can try.**

1. **Take yourself out to eat in your favorite restaurants.** I used to be so uncomfortable being alone with myself. Then, one day, I decided to go beyond my comfort zone. I ate in my favorite restaurant alone. It was a breakthrough experience for me. Treat yourself after hard work days, and take yourself to a nice dinner.

2. **Spend time in nature.** According to research, spending time in nature is good for your health. In addition, it's good for your mind and your spirit. I

like to hug trees. Someone told me that trees would absorb negative energy and release positive energy. I love to be surrounded by trees and greenery to refresh my mind and spirit.

3. **Travel Alone.** Where do you want to go? Go there on your own. Explore that place and meet new friends along the way.

4. **Watch a movie on your own.** Is there a movie you want to watch and there is no one who wants to go with you? Then, you go on your own. Watch the film and enjoy it.

5. **Learn something new, a new skill, or a new hobby.** Discover some of your strengths and gifts by learning something new. Have fun with it. Who knows where these new skills and hobbies can take you.

6. **Take a hot bath.** Take the time to relax and invigorate yourself, taking a nice hot bath. Perhaps you have another way of unwinding. Take that time.

7. **Pray and meditate.** Spending time in prayer and meditation comes with great benefits. It will reduce stress and improve physical, mental, and spiritual health. Include prayer and meditation as part of your activities when you spend time alone with yourself.

Spending time alone opens the door to self-awareness and self-knowledge that will help you reach your full potential. With practice, you can be great company for yourself. Instead of avoiding yourself, discover yourself.

Day 14 Adventure:

For your adventure, spend time alone with yourself. Here is what you need to do.

1. Identify what you want to do when you spend time with yourself—for example, prayer, meditation, a hot bath, or starting a new hobby.
2. Block the time in your calendar when you will do it, and you can start small, like 10 minutes a day.
3. Do it. Go and spend time with yourself.

4. Don't forget to have fun!
5. Journal your experience.

_____

_____

_____

_____

_____

_____

_____

_____

Enjoy the time alone today. You deserve this time. Give this time as your present for yourself.

Day 15. Accept All the Compliments That Come Your Way

"You have to love yourself, or you'll never be able to accept compliments from anyone." Dean Wareham

What's your response when someone compliments you? Are you grateful and believe what they said, or skeptical and uncomfortable?

One day, a friend complimented me on my dress. Instead of being grateful for what she said, I felt embarrassed and uncomfortable. I immediately deflected her compliment by saying, "Oh, this dress is nothing. It was so cheap. I bought it from Goodwill for $5." I also used to think that when someone complimented me, they were fooling around or wanted something from me. Maybe they needed a favor.

Does this sound like you, too? When you're short on self-love, it's not easy to accept compliments. You will feel awkward or skeptical when someone compliments you. You will not believe their words of appreciation. How could you, when you don't see that in yourself?

But, what are compliments and why should we allow ourselves to receive them? Merriam-Webster Dictionary defines compliment as "an expression of esteem, respect, affection, or admiration." Therefore, a compliment is not about what you see in yourself but what others see in you. When you don't love yourself, you only see what is not good about you or what is lacking. Therefore, you will consciously or unconsciously reject other people's expressions of praise and appreciation for you.

Here are the different ways you reject compliments.

  1. Deflect the compliments. When you deflect compliments, you minimize, downplay, redirect the praise or attribute it to luck.

2. Return to the giver. You pass the compliment to the one who complimented you. For example, when someone says that your hair looks beautiful. Instead of saying thank you, you will say, "Not as beautiful as yours."

3. You play the fool. You feel so uncomfortable about the complement that you make a joke about it.

4. Immediate subject alteration. You quickly change the topic. For example, when a coworker compliments your dress, you immediately change the subject by asking what other things you need to do.

5. You are being skeptical. You question the motive of the person who compliments you. You think that they want something from you. For example, someone says you look gorgeous. Your response right away is to ask them what they need from you.

Are you uncomfortable receiving compliments?

The following could be responsible for what you feel. Reflect on these and see which one resonates with you the most.

1. **Low self-esteem.** Some people don't see their value or worth as a person. They think they're not good enough. They're not beautiful enough. So they don't believe the compliments given to them.

Tell yourself you are enough and start working on yourself to increase your self-esteem.

2. **They have trust issues.** Some may have had an unpleasant experience that made them skeptical about compliments. Maybe they experience their boundaries being violated. Hence, when someone gives them compliments, their reaction is, "What do you want from me?"

Also, some Individuals who experience abandonment, betrayal, broken promises, and needs that were not met especially in their childhood could have trust issues.

If you have trust issues, you need to start developing that trust by being trustworthy yourself first. Take baby steps. For example, follow through on what you promise to yourself and to others.

3. **The compliment is disproportionate to their self-image.** The commendation others give you does not align with what you think about yourself. For example, when someone tells you you're beautiful and don't see yourself as beautiful, you will feel uncomfortable and skeptical about that compliment.

Change how you think about yourself. Practice self-affirmation. When you want to learn more on how you could change your self-image, join my Self-Love Mastery: Unlock and Love Your Authentic Self program.

4. **Perfectionism.** Perfectionists have very high expectations of themselves. When someone compliments them on things that the perfectionists don't perceive as perfect, they will reject the compliments.

Perfectionism is hard to achieve and it is also subjective. It depends on the perception of other people. Accept the compliments of others because what you are doing is perfect in their opinion.

5. **They are caught by surprise.** The author and international speaker, Christopher Littlefield talks about the surprise factor of compliments. According to him, when you hear a compliment, the brain needs to process the praise you hear. You deflect the compliments as an initial reaction.

In this case, don't say a lot of words, but simply smile and say 'thank you."

How do you increase your comfort level in receiving compliments?

1. Understand that the compliment is not about you, rather it is about the giver. When someone compliments you, they see something special about you. It is also their way of giving you encouragement and support. For some, it is an expression that they care about you and makes them happy. Accept their expression of admiration and accept their compliments.

2. Understand that what is beautiful and what is good is in the eyes of the beholder. If you don't feel beautiful or that you've done something well, and someone admires you regardless, believe them. In their eyes, you are beautiful and doing good things.

3. Be grateful for what you have. Always look for what is good in your life and express gratitude for them as this will help train your mind to accept other people's expressions of admiration for you. Gratitude will elicit that feeling of goodness and joy. When you are grateful, your brain releases the feel-good hormones like dopamine and serotonin. When you feel good about yourself and your life, it is easier to accept compliments.

4. Acknowledge your strengths and gifts. You have special abilities that other people can admire. Identify your skills, capabilities, and unique talents. Ask your close friends or family members if you struggle to find what is good about you. I am sure that they can tell you something amazing about you.

5. Give yourself affirmation. Learn to affirm yourself. What do you have that you can be proud of? Tell yourself that you are worthy and deserve the compliments they give you. Embrace the fact that you are perfect as you are. Knowing that you're imperfectly perfect will help you realize that whatever they say to you is appropriate.

6. Practice makes you better at receiving compliments. Receiving compliments is a skill that needs training so you will be comfortable with it. Don't say a lot of things when you are surprised when someone gives you compliments. Don't deflect, don't change the topic, don't play the fool, don't ask what they need. Instead, smile at them and say, "Thank you." That's all you have to do.

Day 15 Adventure:

For your adventure today, you must receive all compliments coming your way.

Become aware when you feel uncomfortable. When you are about to reject any compliments, take the following steps.

1. Take a deep breath.
2. Count 1,2,3
3. Smile and say, "Thank you."
4. Silently affirm yourself and tell yourself you deserve all the compliments that come your way.
5. Journal your experience and capture how you feel when you accept compliments.

_____

_____

_____

_____

_____

_____

Day 16. Admire Your Body

"When you're different, sometimes you don't see the millions of people who accept you for what you are. All you notice is the person who doesn't."
- Jodi Picoult, Change of Heart

Imagine you are standing in front of a magic mirror. This mirror will reflect what you think about yourself. What do you see? Do you like your reflection in the mirror, or do you despise it? What are you thinking about your body right now? Maybe so many things come to your mind looking at your body. Perhaps you're looking at the wrinkles on your forehead, uneven skin tones, or a pimple. Maybe you're looking at your flat chest, bulging stomach, or flabby arms. Maybe you hate yourself because you don't have the body of that supermodel you admire. Perhaps you wish to have the perfect face, the perfect eyes, the perfect lips, and the perfect nose.

Some people criticize their bodies and use derogatory words to describe parts of their bodies. They will call their faces stupid. Some even physically hurt their bodies. They punish their bodies for not being the way they want them to be.

There was a point in my life when I hated my body. First, my brother called me an ugly duckling. Then, my mother's friend thought I was my mom's sister, making me think I looked older than my age. Then, a friend compared me to my sister and told me that my sister was prettier than me. All these remarks made me believe that I was ugly. When I looked in the mirror, I found the parts of my body that I believed made me unattractive; like my flat nose, the uneven shape of my eyes, and so forth. As a result, I criticized my face often.

My body image has changed since I learned to love myself. Then I started to see that I am beautiful and perfect as I am.

When your reflection in the magic mirror causes you to hate yourself even more because all you see are negatives, I want you to step back. Close your eyes, hug yourself, and tell yourself you are the image and likeness of God. You are perfect and beautiful as you are. Then, look at the mirror again with that perspective-you are perfect and beautiful. Start transforming your body image by admiring your beautiful body, the vessel of God.

One of the steps you can take to change your perspective about your body is to *transform your negative feelings about your body by being grateful for the function of each part.* For example, if you don't like the shape of your nose, instead of calling it names, say words of gratitude for what the nose does for you. You can say, *"Thank you, my nose, for I can't breathe without you."* Then, give words of appreciation to every part of your body. Consider the things your body can do that you take for granted, like your ability to see, hear, smell, touch, taste, walk and talk, and other amazing things your body can do. Be mesmerized by your body's ability. Doing so makes it easier for you to love and admire your body and look beyond what you think is imperfect.

My journey to self-love started by giving affirmations to my body. When I admire every part of my body that God has given me, I see changes in the way I view myself. The magic mirror reflects a new image of me—a happy, confident me who is comfortable in my own skin. *Start admiring your body.*

You may have a bulging belly, wrinkles on your face, have gray hair, or your body may not look like the celebrities and models you've seen on screen. Perhaps your health is not that great. However, your body can still do some fantastic things.

Day 16 Adventure:

For your adventure today, admire your body.

Try the Magic Mirror Exercise. Please use a full-length mirror if you have one. Otherwise, you can use a mirror you have.

1. Stand in front of the full-length mirror. Take three deep breaths.
2. Close your eyes and get back to your normal breathing.

3. Hug yourself and tell yourself, "I love you. You are perfect as you are."
4. When you are ready, open your eyes and tell your magic mirror to show you your perfect self. "Magic mirror, show me my perfect self."
5. Speak words of gratitude for the things your body can do and does for you starting from your head to your feet.
6. Finally, when you are all done. Hug yourself again and thank God for giving you a fantastic body.
7. How do you feel after doing the exercise? Write your answer in your journal or the space below.

_____

_____

_____

_____

_____

_____

_____

Day 17. Do That Thing You've Always Wanted to Do

"Doing what you want to do is life" –Wallace D. Wattles

Are there things you really want to do but keep putting off because you have no time for them or feel guilty about doing them?

Permit yourself to do that thing you've always wanted to do. Splurge on yourself a little today. Maybe you've wanted to get a massage, learn how to play the piano, take that nature trip, begin a new hobby, change jobs, or move to another place.

Today, spend a little time and think about it. Then, go out and make it happen. If you need to wait for the weekend, make concrete plans for your activity and stick to them.

Identify the things you've been wanting to do but keep putting off for a variety of reasons.

Perhaps your reason is that you feel guilty spending your limited time and money for yourself. You think you are selfish if you put your needs before your loved ones. Maybe you don't think your needs are as important as your loved ones.

Please change your mindset in this area. The truth is you are happier when you can do your desired activities. It will give you a sense of fulfillment. You are more productive and can do more for the people you love when you are happy. Also, doing what you love lowers your stress level, which means a healthier and more pleasant you around other people.

How can you address the no time and no money issue? The following are some of the tips.

1. List down all the things that you love to do. Then, identify those that you really, really, really love to do. When you feel emotionally charged for it, the greater your willpower to make it happen.

2. Have a plan. Visualize that you are doing what you love to do. What does it look like in your mind? What sort of things do you need to enjoy the experience fully? Do you have companions or are you doing it alone? Use your senses in your imagination. Then, from there, create your goals and plan of action to do what you've always wanted.

3. Block your calendar. Once you determine what you will do and when you will do it, put it on your calendar. Protect that time. Trust me; there will be many circumstances that will come your way that will pose as your excuse for not doing it.

4. Start doing what you can afford now. From your list, identify the things that you can do right now that are affordable. For example, maybe there is a movie that you want to watch. It might be streaming somewhere for free or for a fraction compared to watching it in the theater. Then, schedule the time you will watch the movie and protect that time. If you are going on a trip, let's say, three months from today, what are the things you need on that trip that you can afford to buy now. This act will also give you a sense of accomplishment, inspiring you to get on that trip.

5. Save for it. Set aside a percentage of your monthly income that is intended for the things you love to do. For example, if you have a trip that you want to take, create a travel bucket or a travel jar in which you will put perhaps 5% of your income for your trip.

6. Look for a budget way of doing what you love. Check out cheap flights or less expensive hotels and inns in the area where you want to go.

Beautiful you, again, I want to tell you, "If there is a will, there is a way."
You can make things happen when you see them in your mind's eye because when you are doing something that you always wanted to do, it will improve your sense of joy, and sense of meaning.

Day 17 Adventure:

So for your adventure today, do the things you've always wanted to do or plan for it.

Here is what you will do.

  1. List down what you wanted to do.

  _____
  _____
  _____
  _____
  _____
  _____

  2. Pick up one or two things you can do from your list today.

  _____
  _____
  _____
  _____

  3. Open your planner or if you don't have a planner, look at the clock and on a sticky note, write down the time that you will do that thing you've wanted to do and place it somewhere you can see it.
  4. Block that time and when that time comes, you do it.

  _____
  _____

  5. Journal your experience. How do you feel doing the thing you love to do?

  _____
  _____
  _____
  _____
  _____

Day 18. Nourish Your Body

"Tell me what you eat, and I will tell you what you are." -Anthelme Brillat-Savarin

What are you eating every single day?

One of the many ways you can express love for yourself is to be mindful of what we put in your bodies. Food affects your mood, energy, health, focus, cravings, and overall well-being. If you want to know how food affects you, become aware of how your body feels after eating. You can start a food journal.

Our society nowadays is exposed to different kinds of food. Sometimes it is overwhelming. There are various diets and experts have different opinions about food. These experts will tell us what we should and should not eat and, in many cases, these recommendations change based on the expert. But, you know what, you are the expert of your body. You can tell what is good and bad for yourself if you listen to your body.

Your body is a laboratory. The first time I heard about my body being a laboratory was from one of my modules at the International Association of Wellness Professionals when I took my certification to be a wellness coach. When you're discovering what's good for your body, think of your body as a laboratory. Experiment with the foods and drinks that enter your body. Gather data. In your data gathering, include variables like the time of the day you eat a particular food and pay attention to their effects on your body. Next, record how your body feels, your energy level, and any discomfort. For example, did you get acid reflux, headaches, and/or stomach aches.

Increasing your awareness of the effects of food on your body will help you realize that you cannot just follow any diet or food fads. The reason being is what is good for others may not be suitable for you, or what will work for others may not work for you.

We constantly seek balance in our life, including in our food.

How are you going to seek balance for the food element?

    1. Let go of your food rules. If you are eating the same diet every day, your body will get used to it, and you might not remember the first response your body had when you ate a particular food. For example, the fast-food you are eating. You might not remember that the first time you introduced that food to your body, you had constipation and felt bloated or gassy. Try eliminating one or two of the foods you eat daily and replace them with healthier options. See how your body feels with the changes.

    2. **Try new food.** Sometimes the food you've been telling yourself is best for your body isn't really good for your body. Try something new. You might discover a better alternative to what you're eating right now. For example, I use Teff, an African flour, instead of regular flour for my pancakes or other baked goods. Teff is naturally rich in iron, which I needed when I had a very low iron count.

    3. **Try an elimination diet.** The elimination diet will help you identify what food in your regular diet has adverse effects on you. As I mentioned earlier, when you are used to a particular diet, your body is used to its reaction. It will become normal for you.

    4. **Increase your whole food diet.** Whole food is organically, ethically, sustainably, and responsibly produced food. These are foods that have no chemicals, no hormones, or antibiotics and are produced using methods that get all the nutrition that our body needs. Increase your intake of more nutritious food.

    5. **Practice mindfulness when you are eating.** Slow down and notice what you're putting in your mouth and how you eat. When you are eating, chew your food. Be mindful of the taste, texture, and smell of the food. My formator in the convent always reminded me of this habit, that when you eat, you just eat. When you are not consciously eating, it will cause a disconnection between your stomach and your brain. It will take a while for your brain to process what you are eating, leading to overeating, weight

gain, and other problems. Slowing down, consciously choosing the food you eat, and enjoying it, are part of a healthy lifestyle.

What are you eating? Check what's in your refrigerator, cupboard, pantry, and groceries. Evaluate them. Is your food mostly highly processed and loaded with sugar, sodium, and other chemicals?

Day 18 Adventure:

For your adventure today, eat nutritiously.

Here is what you will do.

1. List down the food and drink that you put in your body.
2. Evaluate your list and identify one or two things you're eating that are loaded with sugar, sodium, and preservatives.
3. Find an alternative food that you will eat instead today, or add a healthier option to what you're eating. Maybe you can add a salad for brunch, eat whole grains instead of white bread, or add more fruits to your breakfast.
4. Journal how you feel eating nutritiously.

_____

_____

_____

Show yourself that you love your body by treating it like a queen for a day. Instead of giving in to your regular habits and impulses of eating unhealthy food, eat nutritious food today.

Feel free to continue for the remainder of the month and better yet, for the rest of your life. Your body will thank you for it.

Please consult your doctor, nutritionist or health practitioner before starting a new or elimination diet, especially if you have health problems.

Day 19. Exercise

"The only bad workout is the one that didn't happen." Anonymous

Do you exercise regularly? Why don't you?

Moving your body is one of the best things you can do if you want to be healthy and in a happy mood.

Our body is composed of hundreds of joints and muscles that function very well when you are moving them. Exercise will also help the flow of oxygen in your body, which will make the different systems in your body function better.

Some people don't exercise because they think that exercise is only for those who want to lose weight. This is a myth that I want to debunk right now.

Exercising is not only for those who want to lose weight. The proper exercise will help you feel energetic and young. It also makes you feel happy because your brain will release feel-good hormones like endorphins, serotonin, and dopamine. These hormones will help improve mood and reduce stress. In addition, when you have less stress, you can sleep better and improve your immune system. When you feel good, you will also improve your self-esteem. When you increase your self-esteem, it is easier for you to love yourself.

Hence, exercise is good for your physical and mental health.

Get your exercise gears and start moving your body!

However, to keep moving and motivated to exercise regularly, you need to find the body movements that you enjoy and love to do. Otherwise, you will not be inspired to exercise.

Explore those different ways to move your body and find the one that your body is in tune to do. For example, maybe you like hiking or walking with friends, working out in the gym or at home, or dancing. Explore the different forms of exercise and keep the ones that you enjoy.

I explored different ways to move my body because I quickly got bored. Then, I found that dancing is my thing and I stick to it. I may do some yoga movements in between my dancing. You can do that same thing. Find the mix of different forms of body movements that you love doing.

Suppose you find yourself giving excuses not to exercise, like, no time, exercise is tedious, or there is something better you can do with your time than exercising. In that case, I want you to return to your goals and desired life and see how proper exercise can get you to the life you want.

Then, turn your excuses around. For example, no time, you can find time to do your exercise by blocking it in your calendar. Evaluate your activities and identify those you can replace with exercise.

Be creative. As a teacher, I get my workout by playing with my students on the playground or dancing with them. Identify activities in which you can incorporate some of your body movements. Perhaps, while watching TV, you can do some stretching, walking, or running in place instead of just sitting.

Maybe you have limited movement. Perhaps parts of your body are in pain, fractured, or paralyzed for any reason. Ask for guidance from professionals like your occupational or physical therapists, doctor, and other health practitioners on how to exercise or move your body safely.

Day 19 Adventure:

For your adventure, start your exercise routine today.

1. Explore the body movements you enjoy so you will keep doing them. List down the type of exercise you want to try. It could be yoga, dancing, or pilates.
2. Pick one of those you want to try that you can do today.
3. Block 30 minutes for exercise in your calendar.
4. Go, move your body!
5. Journal your experience. Pay attention to how you feel.

_____

_____

_____

_____

_____

_____

The following day, you can explore another form of body movement until you find the ones you enjoy the most. You could start exercising two times a week and work up to five times a week.

You can use tracking devices like Fitbit or Apple Watch to remind yourself that it is time for you to move your body. Also, it will inspire you to continue going as you see your little wins when you hit your daily goals.

Have fun moving your body today!

Remember to see your doctor before starting any exercise program, especially if you have chronic health problems like heart diseases, diabetes or arthritis, or any other health concerns.

Day 20. Get Enough Sleep

"Never waste any time you can spend sleeping." – Frank H. Knight.

Do you get enough sleep? Do you wake up feeling refreshed and energetic or tired and still sleepy? One of the problems people face in the modern world is a lack of sleep.

Our world is fast-changing and very stressful. There are many things that can trigger stress and cause sleepless nights. In addition, you have all sorts of distractions like social media, the news on TV, and everything on the internet that keeps you awake even in the middle of the night.

You know that you don't get enough sleep when you wake up in the morning feeling tired, still sleepy, you can't think straight, or cranky. I know that I quickly get angry or irritated when I lack sleep.

The other effects of lack of sleep are struggles with focus and attention. When you're doing important tasks, it affects your accuracy and judgment. Your tasks will take a little longer to finish, thus, affecting your productivity and efficiency. Also, you may get hunger pangs. You feel like you are starving and mess up your metabolism. If you want to lose weight, you need to sleep. You also lack physical and mental energy when you don't sleep.

According to the Sleep Foundation, an adult needs seven to nine hours of sleep per night. Even if you think you only need 4 hours, try giving yourself a full seven for a week and note the changes in how you feel and function. Few things will do more for your health, attitude, and happiness than getting at least seven hours of sleep each night.

Getting enough sleep will help you replenish the energy you lost during the day. It helps you be more focused and attentive. Hence you are more productive, creative, and efficient with whatever you do.

Sleep will give you a healthier heart, lower your blood pressure, and boost your immune system.

Maybe you said, yeah, I hear you. I know the impact of sleep on my health, but I struggle with sleep.

I understand. I also had difficulty sleeping because I used to take home my unfinished work. I was prone to stress. Little things used to cause me to feel stress, which kept me awake at night as I could not get things out of my mind.

What will you do if you can't sleep? Here are some things that you can try.

1. Create a sleep routine. Having a routine will help signal your body that it is time to sleep. Plan a sleep time and turn off your television and other electronic devices sixty to ninety minutes before your planned time. For example, if you plan to sleep at 9:00 pm, turn off your electronics no later than 8:00 pm. The blue light emitted from electronic devices will disrupt your sleep pattern. Take this time as your calming down moment. You could turn on sleeping meditation music, dim the light, pray, meditate, do some journaling, or drink a calming tea like chamomile tea or lavender.

2. **Do not fight your thoughts when you can't sleep.** When you have unfinished business or something is stressing you out that causes your thoughts to be active while in bed, don't try to eliminate them. When you fight with your thoughts by trying to stop them, the more they will intensify. Instead, get up and write those things down and tell yourself you'll take care of them tomorrow. Writing them down will help release your worries. Then, when you go back to bed, do some breathing exercises. Focus on your breath. Follow the rise and fall of your belly. It helps when you repeat a word as a mantra. For example, as a Christian, I say Jesus as I breathe in and Christ as I breathe out. You can also use love or peace, whatever makes you feel comforted. Just make it short, maybe a maximum of two words. Your thoughts will go away like clouds when you don't engage with them.

3. **Journal your experience for that day and release your anxiety, worry, fear, excitement, and whatever emotions you have.** In your journal, you can also include things you are grateful for that day. There is no better way to end your day than to say words of gratitude. It will relax your mind and help release feel-good hormones so that you can turn-in happy and calm.

4. **Do some breathing exercises before sleeping.** Deep breathing will help you release tension in your body that has accumulated over the course of the day. When our body is tense, it hinders our ability to sleep. You can try progressive relaxation techniques when you have no muscle pain or joint problems. The progressive relaxation techniques will help you relax your muscle group by slowly tensing and then relaxing each muscle group. You can start from your feet to your head. As you breathe in, you tighten the target muscle group. Then, hold it for 7 seconds and relax that particular muscle group. You can do other breathing exercises to help you release the day's tension and anxiety.

Sometimes the best thing you can do to express love for yourself is going to bed.

Day 20 Adventure:

So for your adventure today, Reflect and Write in your journal.

1. How many hours do you sleep at night? Is this number of hours enough for you? How do you feel when you wake up in the morning? You have enough sleep when you wake up refreshed, well-rested, and alert. However, you lack sleep when you wake up in the morning still tired, feel sleepy during the day, and lack energy.

_____

_____

_____

_____

_____

_____

_____

_____

2. If you don't get enough sleep, what steps will you take to get enough sleep today? List those steps.

_____

_____

_____

_____

_____

_____

_____

3. Tonight, you will do what you plan in number 2.

4. Answer the following question on the next day.

How do you feel about having enough sleep?

_____

_____

_____

_____

_____

_____

_____

Day 21. Ask Someone for a Favor

"Be STRONG enough to stand alone, SMART enough to know when you need help, and BRAVE enough to ask for it." -Unknown

Are you comfortable asking for a favor?

One indication that you need to develop self-love is you are not comfortable asking for help. On the conscious level, you may have reasons why you don't ask for a favor. Perhaps your reason is you can do it on your own, or you can do it better than others. But on the unconscious level, your reason could be your fear of rejection.

You might have experienced rejection growing up from your parents or friends. You are hurt. You refuse to ask for a favor to protect yourself from more pain.

Your fear of rejection makes you think you don't want to bother other people. You might refuse to ask for help because you have limiting beliefs that you are not worthy and valuable. Why would people give you their time?

Refusing to ask for help when you really need it is a mask you put on your face, so people will not see your vulnerability. It is a facade to show that you are in control even if you are falling apart inside.

What is that one thing you need to believe about yourself to accept help from others?

I know you are willing to help others when someone asks for help because it will make you feel good. Right?

Asking for help is not just about you. It is also for the people who are willing to give you support. Do not deprive other people of experiencing the joy of helping you. Allow them to help you so you can make them happy as well. Ask for a favor.

But what if they say "No?" I know that will trigger your fear of rejection. But before you allow your feelings to spiral and be upset and resent those who said, "No," I want you to take a deep breath and reflect on your life's situation. YOU CAN'T SAY YES TO ALL THE REQUESTS FROM THE PEOPLE YOU CARE ABOUT. No matter how much you try. There are times that you have to say "NO," too. Please don't make it a big deal or take it personally when other people don't help you when you need help. They have their reasons. Look for another person who is available to help you. Just ask for it.

If you regularly help others, it is reasonable for you to assume that others will help you.

Have mercy on yourself. Don't force yourself to carry an unnecessary burden. Asking for help will help lighten your loads. It is nice to know that someone out there cares about you as they extend their hands to help you. Better relationships are formed when there is a balance between giving and receiving.

Remember, you're important and deserve help when you need it.

Day 21 Adventure:

For your adventure today, ask for help.

Here's what you will do.

1. Think of your tasks with which you could use some support. List down those things.
2. Next to each item on your list, put the name of the person you think can assist you with it.
3. Pick one task. Then go to that person you think can help you.
4. Journal your experience. Pay attention to how you feel.

_____

_____

When you are not used to asking someone for a favor, start small and build your comfort level.

Day 22. Express Gratitude

'A Grateful Heart is a Magnet for Miracles' — Jane Fuller

What is it about your life that makes you feel grateful?

Being grateful is seeing the good things in your life, even amid hardship and difficulties. You are grateful when in the dark night of your soul, you still see a tiny spark of light and are thankful for it.

We are typically drawn to negativities and notice the things that are not working in our lives. We see what is missing rather than appreciate what we already have. We tend to focus on our limitations and weaknesses instead of our gifts and strengths.

You are in the majority when you tend to see bleakness, problems, or what is lacking in your life because our brains are wired that way for survival. For our ancestors to survive in the wild, they needed to anticipate the worst to better prepare for it. Even if we are not in the wild anymore, we still revert to our ancestors' way of staying alive.

Oprah Winfrey says, *"What you focus on expands, and when you focus on the goodness in your life, you create more of it."*

When you focus on the negativities, you attract most of them, and negative experiences become your reality. But when you focus on what is good and worthwhile, you will create more positivity. Therefore, why not focus on what is fantastic in your life? Why not train your brain to see goodness even amid difficulties? Why not switch your perspective and focus on finding the little things that work in your life?

But how can you be grateful in an environment where it seems like there is no hope?

When you feel like there is nothing to be thankful for, try this Gratitude Exercise.

Close your eyes. Then take three deep breaths. As you breathe in, say these words, "Thank you, God," and as you breathe out, say, "for the good things I am about to see." Then go back to your normal breathing. With your eyes still closed, think of that one thing that makes you happy. No matter how small it is. It could be your child's laughter when you are doing things together, the smell of roses, or your favorite place. Take a picture of it in your mind. Then, expand that image, make it big, and make it clear. Remember the happiness and joy that you felt at that time. Hold that feeling and then express gratitude for everything or every person you see in that picture. You can add more images of what makes you happy as you continue the exercise. Savor that good feeling that you experience.

When you are ready, you can open your eyes. Embrace yourself, and say "Thank you."

Do this Gratitude Exercise regularly to train your mind to see goodness in your life.

This exercise will open up your energy toward gratitude. When you do this, more good things will show up for you because your mind's eyes will start to look for them. Then, you will realize that there are so many things you can be grateful for regardless of whatever challenges you encounter in your life.

If we learn to focus on the things that we are grateful for, the more we will attract them into our lives.

What are the benefits of having a grateful heart?

1. **A grateful heart will help enhance your relationship with yourself, others, and God.** When you are full of gratitude, you acknowledge the help of other people in your life. As a result, you want to develop better relationships with them. If you are a believer in something higher than you, you recognize the hands of the divine that guides you through the ups and downs of your life. Finally,

when you are grateful, you will appreciate your life and what you have, which will deepen your love for yourself.

2. A grateful heart will reduce stress and anxiety.
When you are thankful, your body will release the feel-good hormones, dopamine and serotonin in your body. These chemicals will make you feel happy and relax your body. When you feel good and happy, you cannot have stress and anxiety because they cannot co-exist. When you have less stress, it will also boost your immune system.

3. A grateful heart will improve your social and physical health. When you are grateful, your brain will also release oxytocin. This hormone will want you to build a bond with other people and yourself. When you feel loved and appreciate the care you receive from others, the more you'll want to take care of yourself, leading you to a healthier life.

4. A grateful heart will strengthen your overall mood and sense of wellbeing.
When you are thankful, you uplift your mood and change your state from negative to positive. In addition, it will boost your overall outlook on life, helping you to feel more optimistic about your present and allowing you to see a brighter future. Gratitude allows you to feel more satisfied with your life.

How can you build a gratitude practice?

Gratitude is a habit that you need to cultivate in your life. Include gratitude rituals in your daily routine to increase your gratitude. The following are some steps that you can take to increase gratitude.

1. **Become aware of even the little things.** You can create gratitude habits by noticing the little things that make you feel good. For example, notice at least three things that may seem ordinary to you each day and be thankful for them. These could be when you open your eyes in the morning, the weather, or the food you are eating. Noticing and expressing gratitude for the little and ordinary things in your life will help cultivate gratitude.

2. **Start a gratitude journal.** Write down the things you are grateful for in your life. Everyday look for five things that you experience that you appreciate and enter them in your gratitude journal. Writing down the things you are thankful for will force you to think about and acknowledge what you usually take for granted that adds meaning to your life.

3. **Vocally express words of gratitude.** Please do not keep it to yourself when you feel grateful for something or someone. Instead, tell the person you are thankful for what they have done for you. Say the things you are grateful for because when you hear them, it will help intensify the good feelings and help you want to do it more. You will make other people happy when you acknowledge their contributions to your life.

Building gratitude is a skill that you can develop and improve. The more you do it, the better you will be with it, and it will become automatic.

Day 22 Adventure:

For your adventure starting today, find three things you are grateful for in your life. Then, write them down in your journal. Please include the usual items you see, like water, the air you breathe, the water you drink, your laptop, and anything else you enjoy or value.

Reflect and Write in your journal or the space below.

What are you grateful for in your life right now?

_____
_____
_____
_____
_____
_____
_____

Day 23. Keep a Journal

"Journal writing, when it becomes a ritual for transformation, is not only life-changing but life-expanding." – Jen Williamson

Do you keep a journal?

When you want to love yourself, you need to increase your self-knowledge because it is not easy to love someone you don't know. One of the ways you can increase your knowledge is to practice journaling.

Journaling is an informal way of writing where you record your feelings, thoughts, reflections, and ideas.

I learned so much about myself through journaling. I started journaling in grade school, which I called "Dear Diary."

I started a journal because I feared expressing myself for fear of rejection and judgment growing up. Journaling is one of my ways to release overwhelming emotions. It is my way to clear my cluttered mind and when I want answers to some of my questions. My journal is like my best friend who knows my deepest secrets, fears, and desires and I am confident it will not judge me.

Why is journaling important?

One of the most effective ways to access your subconscious mind and bring your unconscious tendencies to your consciousness, is JOURNALING. For example, maybe you have questions about your behavior. You don't understand why you are easily annoyed by a particular behavior or what is the real reason why you can't keep a job or relationship? Journaling might be able to help you find answers to your questions so that you can understand your behavior.

Journaling will help you see the patterns or habits affecting your current situation. When you examine what you've entered in your journal, a pattern might emerge that will hint at what you need to change or continue doing in your life.

Journaling will help you express the emotions that you can't vocally express at the moment, especially when they are very raw emotions. Sometimes we need to hold our words and feelings because we don't know how they will affect us and others. Writing them in your journal will help you sort those feelings and become more objective or rational with the situation that triggers your intense emotions.

Journaling will allow you to record your experiences and the lessons you learned that could be helpful for you in the future. For example, I had a struggle that I encountered, and I asked myself how I would get through it. Then, I stumbled upon my old journal. While reading the journal, I was grateful to find the answer to my question. I saw the process of how I overcame similar obstacles. It gave me insight into what I could do with my current issue, and it inspired me, that if I did it before, I could do it again.

In journaling, you are allowing yourself to express what it is that you hide inside. As a result, you can uncover the authentic self that you may have suppressed for a long time. It is very therapeutic as you permit yourself to be you.

I urge you to start journaling today.

Here are some journaling techniques you can use to learn more about yourself by keeping a journal.

1. **Make journaling a habit.** Start small when you're just starting the journaling practice. Little wins each day will boost your desire to keep going. For example, you may begin by writing three things you are grateful for each day. Set aside 5-20 minutes each morning or evening to write in your journal.

2. **Review your life experience.** Writing your life experiences will help you see your patterns, tendencies, victories, and obstacles that you overcame. When you record them, you can learn from them and marvel at your

progress over the years. In addition, you will also be amazed by the new perspective you uncover when you review your journal.

3. **Use writing prompts.** There are books of journaling prompts. Journaling prompts are questions you can ask yourself, and then write your responses to them. The following are sample questions to help you get started.

I know I love myself because...
What habits do I need to change so I will have less stress?
What is my ideal life?
If I could start over, I would...

4. **Timeline Journaling.** You need to block 30 minutes or more for this type of journaling because you will reflect and record your thoughts about your life. For example, write about your home life, achievements, or what you have loved doing since you were a child. How have you ended up where you are? How have your perceptions and understanding of life changed over the years? What do you want to change going forward?

Timeline Journaling is a powerful tool to uncover your purpose in life and understand the root cause of your limiting beliefs.

5. **Conscious/Subconscious Journaling.** I love this journaling strategy. You can use this if you have questions that you want answers to from your inner depths or higher self. Get a piece of paper or a page of your journal and fold it in half. Then label the left side conscious and the right-side subconscious. On the conscious part, write your question that needs an answer. Then, close your eyes. Take a deep breath and ask the question again in your mind. Continue following your breath as you allow your mind to calm down. After a minute or so, open your eyes and write down everything that comes to mind under the subconscious part of your paper. When done, read what you have written, and you'll find the answer to your question, or you will have insight that will help you with your situation.

Spending time in silence and journaling is one way you express love for yourself. However, one important thing you should remember when you write in your journal is **DO NOT CENSOR IT.**

Write everything. It is very therapeutic.

Journaling is intimidating for most people. Many don't want to look at the dark places in their lives or are afraid that they may uncover something they don't want to see. However, if you want to be empowered, you need to shed light on the dark spaces of your life. Only when you know and face your shadows can you experience inner freedom. Journaling will help reveal so much about you that you can improve your life and achieve your goals.

A life worth living is worth recording. Your life is important enough to write down. Whether you do it by hand or with a word processor is up to you.

Day 23 Adventure:

For your adventure today, spend a few minutes recording events, your thoughts and feelings of your day. If you are already in the habit of journaling, try one of the strategies suggested. You could try conscious/subconscious journaling. Write in your journal or the space below.

_____

_____

_____

_____

_____

_____

_____

_____

_____

_____

_____

Day 24. Stop Seeking for Validation

"I can't tell you the key to success, but the key to failure is trying to please everyone."
—Ed Sheeran.

Is your desire for approval hurting You?

To love yourself, you need to like yourself. You will like yourself if you believe in yourself. When you believe in yourself, you will stop the need to seek approval from others.

Insecurity and the desire for approval can damage your life, relationships, and future. This deep-seated desire to please people is difficult to eliminate, but you can do this.

Approval seeking is one of my struggles in life. I suppressed what I felt and thought because of my fear of rejection. I had self-doubt. I didn't believe in myself. Because I was always unsure, I looked to people in authority to give me a nudge or a signal to do something and even what to feel.

One of the reasons why people constantly seek approval is their limiting beliefs about themselves.

Limiting beliefs are thoughts or opinions that you believe are true that stopped you from going after your dreams or goals. They are the reasons why you have self-doubts. For example, maybe you think you are not good enough, too young, or too old. If you want success in your life, eliminate your limiting beliefs and become unstoppable. You don't have to wait for others to approve of you because you already gave yourself approval. Remember your Creator already approves of you.

Empower yourself to stake a claim in your own life. Believe in yourself because when you believe in yourself, other people cannot pressure you into doing anything you don't want to, and no one can hold you back from doing something you know you can do.

People can label you, put you in a box, and tell you who you are and what you are capable of, but no one can know you as you know yourself. Increase your self-awareness, you will know who you really are.

If you want to be free from constantly seeking the approval of others, follow these following steps.

1. **Realize that disapproval is a way for others to get what they want.** People may disapprove of your opinion because they want theirs to prevail, or they will disapprove of your clothing, hairstyle, or anything else because of their beliefs or perceptions.

2. **Be aware that the world will not end when someone disapproves of you.** We seem to be born with an intense desire to fit in. But what happens when someone disapproves of you? Nothing. The world will continue moving. The sun will continue to shine. Our negative thoughts about other people's disapproval of us are the ones that cause the feeling of anxiety or embarrassment, but like everything else, it shall pass if you don't put your focus on it.

3. **Take care of yourself.** If you're constantly seeking approval, you're not taking good care of yourself. Show yourself that you're valuable by focusing some of your time and energy on yourself. Do something that you enjoy doing. Treat yourself and explore your passions, talents, and gifts.

4. **Fill your life with what is essential.** Identify what is important and what you value the most in your life. What makes you happy, and what makes you feel fulfilled? When you know what they are, you don't need to seek approval from others.

5. **Express what you think and feel about something.** Give your opinion, even if it makes you uncomfortable. Start with more minor things. Do you prefer black or red? Which movie would you like to see? What do you want to eat for lunch?

Being overly concerned about the opinions of others is damaging to your self-esteem. Whenever you seek approval, you're telling yourself that you don't matter and diminish your importance.

Know that you matter, and your opinion is as valuable as theirs. Allow your individuality to be seen and experienced by others. There is only ONE of you in the world, and if you become what others want you to be, the world will miss the gifts only you can give.

If you want to learn more about how you could increase your self-confidence and eradicate limiting beliefs, join our Self-Love Mastery: Unlock and Love Your Authentic Self. In this program, you will learn how to embrace your authentic self to stop the approval-seeking habit.

Day 24 Adventure:

For your adventure today, stop seeking approval.

Reflect and write in your journal or the space below.

  1. How does your approval-seeking behavior affect your life?

  _____

  _____

  _____

  _____

  2. Write the steps you can take to stop approval-seeking behavior. Then circle one step you can take today to free yourself from constantly seeking approval.

  _____

  _____

  _____

  _____

3. Journal your experience. Pay attention to how you feel doing things or ecisions without asking for approval.

_____

_____

_____

_____

It is ok if your idea is different from others or if you're different from others. Everyone who loves you will still love you. Do not feel weary or sad when anyone leaves you because they disapprove of you. They don't belong to your life.

Day 25. Be in the Moment

Are you living in the present, past or future?

I had this habit of always rushing to things. I like to multitask, my mind was always thinking about what I had to do next on my to-do list. My mind would wander when I went out with my friends or loved ones. It went somewhere else so that I missed the opportunity to get to know them better and enjoy their company. I later regretted this.

When I joined the convent to become a nun, my formator saw me eating my breakfast. She said, *"Dolly, when you eat, just eat."* I looked at her confused and asked her what she meant. She told me that I was sitting on the edge of the chair. My body showed I was in a hurry. My mind was not on what I was doing at that time, eating breakfast.

I tried to explain to her the important things I needed to finish. She asked me these questions that made me stop and reflect. If you were on your deathbed, can you say you lived your life well? Can you say you have no regrets because you savored each moment? Well, my answer to those questions was "No." How could it have been anything else? I couldn't always remember what I did the day before, but my frustration and pain was always easily recalled.

Then my formator said, you can't completely enjoy your life, and you will miss a lot if you don't live the moment. Savor the experience. *JUST BE.* Again she told me that when you eat, you just eat. Savor the taste of the food, feel its texture, and chew your food properly. It is good for your senses and your digestion.

Many people are in the habit of not living in the moment. Their minds and hearts are living in the past or the future. When they are with their family, their mind is at work, thinking about the projects they must finish. When they are at work, they are thinking about their planned family vacation. Hence, they don't enjoy the present moment.

Some are always in a rush because they are always in a hurry to move on. They haven't paid close attention to their present actions. Hence, they forget something, get stressed out, and don't enjoy the moment.

You might be one of these people. You are always on the go and forget to take pleasure in and relish the moment.

Today, I urge you to practice mindfulness. Be in the moment.

Mindfulness is about becoming aware of your outer world. For example, how does the book or device you are holding right now reading this adventure feel? It is becoming attentive to what is going on in your world, how it affects you, and how you affect the world around you.

Being mindful and living in the moment comes with great benefits. Research shows that it will help lower your stress and anxiety. In addition, it will improve your self-confidence and self-esteem as you become more aware of what you put in your mind and body. Also, it will increase your beliefs about yourself and your confidence as you uncover more of your gifts and potential.

When you want to develop self-love, you need to learn to live in the moment and be mindful of what you allow in your space and what you project into the world. Practice mindfulness today.

Day 25 Adventure:

For your adventure, do a mindfulness exercise. The following is a less than 5-minute mindfulness exercise you can practice to start your mindfulness habit. This exercise is designed to cultivate heightened awareness and appreciation of simple daily tasks.

Mindful Awareness Exercise

This exercise aims for you to spend time paying attention to what you're doing daily instead of going through the motions on autopilot.

1. Think of a task that you routinely do every day. Something that you don't think about when you do it because it is automatic for you. For example, washing dishes, typing on the computer, taking a shower, or eating.

2. Take a moment to notice the object you're using to do the job. For instance, when you are eating. Notice what your food looks like and its smell. Pay attention to the texture of the food and how it feels when it gets to your mouth. Savor the taste of the food and chew your food slowly.

3. Notice how you feel as you do the task. Are you excited? Anxious? Happy?

4. Take a moment to appreciate the parts of your body that enable you to do the task. Say words of gratitude for those parts.

5. Take a deep breath. Release a positive intention on what you want to experience as you continue with what you are doing.

Journal your experience. How do you feel after doing this exercise?

_____
_____
_____
_____
_____
_____
_____
_____
_____

Day 26. Pray and Meditate

"In the attitude of silence, the soul finds the path in a clearer light, and what is elusive and deceptive resolves itself into crystal clearness. Our life is a long and arduous quest after Truth."-Mahatma Gandhi

Do you spend time in prayer and meditation? If you said, "No" or "Sometimes," I urge you today to pray and meditate.

Why is it essential to cultivate prayer and meditation?

When you want to develop self-love, you must connect to your inner depths and your Creator, who holds your blueprint. Prayer and meditation are the best ways to communicate within and to the Spirit of God, your Creator.

I came to know more about myself when I practiced prayer and meditation. I want to reiterate here that self-knowledge is essential to developing self-love. When you spend time in silence, through prayer and meditation, you allow yourself to uncover more about yourself that you can bring to your consciousness. The greater your knowledge about yourself, the more you can access your gifts and talents and understand your tendencies. Hence, it is easier for you to embrace your individuality and achieve your goals and desired life.

What is prayer and meditation?

Prayer is talking to your God. It is an act of faith. You trust and believe that a Being higher than you who knows you in and out is listening to you and will help and guide you in your next steps.

Meditation, on the other hand, is COMING HOME to You. It is going inside you to increase your awareness of your inner world. It is an opportunity for you to see what is blocking your way from achieving your full potential and your strengths to get you to where you want to be. Meditation is when you listen to the promptings of God within you.

Prayer and meditation are accessible to you 24/7.

What are the benefits of prayer and meditation?

1. **They lower stress and anxiety.** Different studies show prayer and meditation reduce stress and anxiety. They help calm down your nervous system. Also, when you pray and meditate, you give your control over to God. That act releases you from too much pressure. In addition, the breathing exercises you do when you pray and meditate can help you relax and calm your mind.

2. **They help improve your physical and mental health.** When you have less stress, you boost your immunity. Hence, you are less susceptible to stress. When you experience inner peace and calm, you lower your blood pressure which can aid in combating heart disease. Prayer and meditation will help improve your focus and concentration.

3. **You are more aware of your thoughts.** When you pray and meditate, you heighten your awareness of thoughts that adversely affect your life. You can have better control of them since you are conscious of them. When you can control your thoughts, you can manage your emotions, feelings, and behavior. That is self-mastery.

4. **You are happier and experience inner peace and calm.** Studies show that people who pray and practice meditation are happier and more at peace because they worry less. You increase your faith and trust that your needs are provided for as you connect to the Divine. Getting in touch with your inner wisdom and guidance will give you a sense of control.

5. **You are more at home with yourself.** When you pray and meditate, you increase your self-awareness and self-knowledge, which will help you love yourself more. When you love yourself, you enjoy your company. Whether

you are alone or with someone, it doesn't make a difference because you are happy and comfortable regardless.

How to get started with prayer and meditation?

You can practice both prayer and meditation at the same time. More often, when you pray, if you allow it, it will lead to meditation. Prayer is two-way communication between you and God; after you express your prayers, you need to spend time in silence. In silence, you will be drawn to meditate.

You need to make a decision that you will pray and meditate. Sometimes you will not feel like doing it but do it anyway. You will be amazed at how you will feel after.

Here are some other tips as you start your prayer & meditation practice.

1. **Include prayer and meditation in your daily routine.** Find the time in your day to spend in prayer and meditation. Although it is good that you can practice prayer without ceasing, spending a few minutes, perhaps 5 minutes, is a good start.

2. **When you come to your prayer and meditation, begin with an effective breathing exercise.** You will know if you are breathing the right way when your belly rises when you breathe in, and it falls when you breathe out. Practice pulling air from your diaphragm, not your upper chest, when you breathe.

3. **Use your breathing like a mantra.** Inhale while you give yourself positive thoughts and feelings. Then, exhale negative thoughts and unpleasant feelings. Breathing will help calm your mind, making it easier for you to connect with your inner self.

4. **Listen to meditation music.** Meditation music or praise and worship songs can put you in a mode for prayer and meditation. Incorporate this in your daily prayer and meditation practice. Listen to praise and worship songs on Youtube or other apps like Apple Music, Spotify, and others.

5. **Do some stretching or yoga poses before you pray or meditate.** Stretching and yoga poses will relax your mind and body. It is easier for you to come into silence when your mind and body are relaxed. Remember to consult your doctor, physical therapist, or other health practitioners before starting a new exercise routine, especially when you have some injury or body pain.

Pray or meditate with others. Join a church or meditate and pray with your friends or family members. My formator once told me to pray and meditate with a group. Doing so will help you get into the right mood for prayer and meditation. The presence of each other will encourage you to continue with the practice, and you are lifting each other in the spiritual realm.

Expect to conquer your anxiety when you start your journey toward personal peace through prayer or meditation. However, this will take time and require consistency--make it a habit.

Day 26 Adventure:

For your adventure today, begin practicing prayer and meditation. Block the time in your schedule.

Remember to journal your experience and how you feel after you pray and meditate.

_____
_____
_____
_____
_____
_____
_____
_____

Experience more joy, calm and inner peace, pray and meditate today

Day 27. Make Plans for Your Future

"If you leave your growth to randomness, you'll always live in the land of mediocrity."
-Brendon Burchard

What is your vision for your future? Do you have plans to get there?

How do you envision yourself 5 or 10 years from now? Do you want to be financially free, visit different countries, or become the best in your field? Then, start creating a plan for it. Start setting your goals and take steps to achieve your goals and desired life. If you love yourself, you will care for yourself, including planning for your future.

According to Brian Tracy, personal development and business coach, *"Only about 3% of Americans make plans for their future, and the other 97% are working for those who make plans and execute them on a daily basis"*.

An interesting fact, isn't it? Maybe you belong to the 97%. Perhaps you have plans but fail to execute them or give up at the first obstacle you encounter.

In achieving your goal, engaging your unconscious mind is vital. According to Matthew Barnett, a neuro-linguistic programming instructor, "Your conscious mind is the goal setter, but your unconscious mind is the goal-getter."

How will you engage your unconscious mind? By attaching emotions to your goals. Here's how.

Visualize your desired life, or the goal you want to achieve. See in your mind's eye what it looks like when you achieve your goals or you are already living your desired life. What are you doing, and who is with you in that life you envision? How do you feel? Intensify those beautiful feelings and take a picture of them in your mind. After your visualization, write down your experience in your journal.

Put a marker on that journal entry, so when you feel down or discouraged while working towards your goal, you can reread that journal entry to inspire you to keep going.

Another way of attaching emotions to your goals is to identify your BIG WHY. The bigger your reason, the greater it is that you will follow through with your goals. We talked about your big why in chapter 1. You can go back to it if you want to review this concept.

When you have your goals, it is time to create a plan--your step-by-step actions to reach your desired outcome, the future that you envisioned. Include in your plan the steps you will take when you encounter obstacles toward your goals to ensure you will not give up immediately.

I have met some people who do not have plans for their future because they don't know if they will still be alive at that time or don't think they have control over the future.

I heard some say, "Why plan ahead? Why not live one day at a time? or "Whatever will be, will be."

I understand that we don't know what will happen tomorrow, and we need to live moment by moment to experience our present fully, but it doesn't give you an excuse to leave your life to chance and mediocrity. If you don't have a plan for your future, someone else will plan it for you or you will be part of someone else's plan.

Maybe you will tell me that God knows your future and He will take you to that future. Why plan? Hear me out. The Bible says you create the plan and God will direct your steps. Though I believe God has a better plan for you, He wants you to take part in that plan. That is the reason we have brains. Otherwise, God would have given us an empty skull.

Day 27 Adventure:

For your adventure today, I invite you to spend time alone with yourself and envision the life that you want in the future. Let your imagination run wild. Create a compelling future. Write them down, then create your big goals. From your big goals, break them down into smaller goals or benchmarks. What steps you will take to get to your goals. Make a plan and do at least one thing daily to make it a reality. That means taking the first step today!

Reflect and write in your journal or the space below.

1. What kind of life do you envision for the future?

_____

_____

_____

_____

_____

2. What step or steps are you going to take today to get to that future?

_____

_____

_____

_____

_____

Day 28. Stop Comparing Yourself with Others

"The only person you should try to be better than is who you were yesterday." – Unknown

Do you find yourself comparing yourself to others? Do you often feel bad about your life due to the comparison? Many people are not content with their life because they constantly compare themselves to others. Unfortunately, with social media, it is easier for us to get into the trap of this comparison habit. It only takes a moment to find yourself wishing you had someone else's career, body, house, or vacation.

I used to live in a comparison cage. I compared myself to my sister and my best friend. I think they are intelligent and beautiful, and there I was, the ugly girl. While in this cage, I felt excited and happy when people who I believed above me encountered misfortune. I thought we were now equals.

Two things may happen when you compare yourself to others. You are either delighted with your life because you are better than others or you feel bad because you are at the bottom of the pile. You don't have what others have.

When you compare yourself with others, your emotions and feelings will be like a roller coaster ride, going high and low, and surprising you at every turn. At one point, you like your life, and then at another point, you hate it.

If you want to feel emotionally stable and be happy with your life, stop comparing yourself with others. Instead, compare your current self to your previous self. How is your weight compared to 6 months ago? How are your finances compared to last year? If you're making progress, congratulate yourself. If your life isn't moving forward, pause and address the situation.

Theodore Roosevelt once said, "Comparison is the thief of joy." Think about that statement and decide if it rings true for you.

Today, please claim your happiness and your sanity. Take a step to stop comparing yourself with other people. Instead, acknowledge what you have and be grateful.

Comparing yourself with others is a habit. But, like any habit, you can change it.

The following are some tips to help you stop the comparison habit.

1. **Watch your thoughts and your words.** When you become aware you're comparing yourself to others, shift your focus immediately to something else. For example, start counting your blessings instead.

2. **Realize that you're on a journey.** You are on a journey to becoming your best self. In this journey, you are learning and creating the life you are meant to live. Your experience is unique, different from others, and independent of what others have accomplished.

My spiritual director once told me that everyone is going to the same place, heaven (however you interpret heaven). Along the way, some find fascinating stuff, they stop and savor what they see. Others encounter blocks and bumps along the way, it takes them longer to get to their heaven. Still, others are learning a better way to reach their destination faster. Wherever you are on your journey, know that you are closer to your destination. Savor where you are now in your journey.

3. **Know that comparing yourself to others is a game that you can't win.** Someone will always have a better house than you, more money, a better body, or a more exciting life. Or someone will be lower in status or have less money. If your happiness depends on what you have or don't have, you are on the losing end.

4. **Be grateful for what you have.** Comparisons emphasize the things you are lacking in your life. But, when you are thankful, you see the essential things you possess. Hence, you feel abundance and are happier. There is no room in your heart to wallow on the things you don't have.

Day 28 Adventure:

For your adventure today, take a step to stop comparing yourself with others.

Here is what you will do.

1. Pay attention to your words and thoughts. Catch yourself when you start comparing yourself with others.

2. Shift your focus immediately and replace your thoughts with something you already have that you are grateful for.

Remember that comparing yourself to others is just a habit; like every habit, it can be changed. When you catch yourself making comparisons with others, turn your mindset around and compare yourself with the you of the past. That way you can celebrate triumphs of any size and recognize your transformation.

Remember that you are perfect as you are and have everything in you to live a happy life.

Day 29. Show Kindness

"I shall pass through this world only once. Therefore, any good I can do or any kindness I can show to any human being, let me do it now. Let me not defer or neglect it, for I shall not pass this way again." --Stephen Grellet

How do you feel when you help someone? Do you feel happy and fulfilled?

An act of kindness is something that costs you nothing but will give you so much joy and fulfillment.

What is kindness?

Kindness is your ability to go beyond your personal interests for the good of others.

You might say that this contradicts what we discussed earlier, that you must prioritize yourself. Looking for other people's good doesn't oppose your expression of self-love. On the other hand, you are expressing the ultimate purpose why you have to love yourself: to love others freely and without condition.

In the Bible, Jesus told his disciples to love others as he loves them (John 15:12). So likewise, we are all called to love and serve other people. As social beings, we need to help and love each other in order for our species to thrive and flourish.

Our world right now mirrors people who have not experienced love for themselves. People are hurting each other and being indifferent. There is so much anger in the world. People want to impose their point of view and beliefs on others. There is a lack of respect and sympathy. Just watch the news, and you will see what I mean.

Some people think they express love for themselves when they stop caring about others and do what makes them happy regardless if they hurt the people who love them.

When you love yourself, you are kind to yourself. You listen to yourself. You are connected to the source of love within you. Hence, the love you feel inside will illuminate because love is energy; when you have so much love, it will overflow to the outside, and others will feel it. When you love yourself, it is easier to understand and be kind to others because you experience it yourself.

The ultimate goal for us to love ourselves is to love others.

Showing our love for others is giving them compassion and kindness. To serve them and extend our hands to them in times of need.

Jesus set this example to his disciples when he washed his disciples' feet during the Last Supper. Then he commanded them also to wash each other's feet. That is serving with love and humility.

What are the benefits of kindness?

1. **You will feel abundant.** An act of kindness to other people will help you see that no matter what you have or how little, you have something you can give. It will help you see that there are other people who are struggling more than you. No matter your circumstances, there is something better about you that you can share with others.

2. **You feel good when you help.** It is the magic of giving. You feel fulfilled and happy when you give. When you show kindness to someone, it triggers your brain to release the feel-good hormone.

3. **You open up more opportunities to receive more good things**. Have you heard the saying, the more you give, the more you receive? I heard several stories about people who are so blessed, and if you look at what they do differently, they give more.

One day, I applied for a teaching job in the Philippines. On the day of my interview and teaching demonstration, I was surprised because no one was there except for a young woman. I told her that I was scheduled for an interview and demonstration. Then, she excitedly asked, "Mam Tampos, do you remember me? I was one of your students. I told everyone no need to interview you. You are hired!" As we talked, I was grateful because she remembered the kindness I showed them as my students.

Proverbs 11:24-25 said that *"Some give freely, yet grow all the richer; others withhold what is due, and only suffer want. A generous person will be enriched and one who gives water will get water."*

4. **It will improve your relationships and sense of belongingness.** When you express kindness to others, people will appreciate you more. It will help develop camaraderie and the feeling of isolation will be less.

5. **Kindness is an expression of gratitude.** The more grateful you are for your life and blessings, the more you are willing to show kindness. When you are thankful for the kindness you receive, the more you will be kind to others. Thus, kindness will keep flowing in your life.

How can you develop kindness to other people?

1. **Start with yourself.** Be gentle and compassionate with yourself, especially when you make mistakes. Realize that mistakes are learning opportunities. When you accept and love yourself as you are, it is easier for you to be kind to other people.

2. **Count your blessings.** What are the things that you are grateful for in your life? Once you start counting your blessings, you will see that you have more than enough to share with other people. Your gratitude will propel you to show kindness to others.

3. **Accept and love yourself as you are.** Many people don't feel that they are loved and accepted as they are. Hence, they tend to be hard on others. However, when you feel loved, you open your hearts to others. Always remember that God loves you as you. Embrace that love, so it is easier for you to understand and empathize with people who are different from you.

4. **Decide to be Kind.** Like everything else, being kind is a decision you must make. Every moment you are given the opportunity to be kind. I know there are times when your act of kindness goes wrong, thus giving you more harm than joy. But understand that this is not the norm. When things like this happen, learn from them, but don't let it hinder you from fully experiencing the joy of helping others.

5. **Pray.** Showing kindness to others and even yourself can be very tough, especially when you have a bad experience doing it. Ask for the grace of God to give you the courage to be kind.

Day 29 Adventure:

For your adventure today, show kindness.

Here is what you will do:

1. Think of a friend, co-worker, or stranger you can make happy or assist.

_____

_____

2. Plan how you can help them. You could cheer them up by giving them flowers and cards or cooking a meal.

_____

_____

3. Act on your plan.

4. Capture your experience and how you feel showing kindness in your journal.

_____

_____

Kindness is one of the Fruits of the Holy Spirit (Galatians 5:22-23). When you give, you feel blessed, and you feel great. You will like yourself more if you can share your gifts and resources with others.

Day 30. Send Yourself a Love Letter

"Send Yourself a Love Letter and then take the time to read it to yourself. Express your heartfelt love to yourself." -Iyanla Vanzant.

Have you tried writing yourself a love letter?

This exercise is perfect as you are about to end this adventure. Today is the time for you to honor and celebrate yourself for taking the 30-day adventure to love yourself. Know that the end of this journey is just the beginning of a more powerful, stimulating, and inspiring passage to deeper self-love.

The first time I wrote a love letter to myself was when I experienced my first broken heart. I wrote to myself like I would write to my best friend. I eventually burned that letter as part of my forgiveness and letting go ritual.

Now, I write letters to myself for inspiration and motivation, to visualize my future, hold myself accountable, and give myself affirmation.

Today, you will write a love letter to express your gratitude for yourself; to inspire yourself to pursue your vision for the future and hold yourself accountable for achieving your desired life.

Here is what you will do.

Imagine you have a perfect friend or partner who loves and accepts you as you are. You trust this person, and believe they know everything about you. You don't hide any secrets from this person. Then, write yourself a letter from that person's point of view. What do you want this person to tell you? What loving words and encouragement do you want to hear from this person? Write a letter that will make you feel happy, energized, and inspired to continue your journey to self-love and become your best self.

Write your letter on a special paper to express your worth and value. Then, put that letter in an envelope addressed to yourself. Next, put it in the mail. If it is not possible for you to send your letter in the regular mail, send yourself an email instead, or even leave a voicemail. It's up to you.

You can also write a letter to yourself that you will read during a specific month or year from the day you wrote it. I love doing this to see my progress and also to inspire me.

When you receive the letter, please keep it where you can access it when you need a dose of encouragement and motivation.

You can turn this into a habit.

Day 30 Adventure:

For your adventure today, write yourself a love letter on special paper and drop it in the mail. Once received, re-read your thoughts and keep your letter in an easily accessible place to read again when you need inspiration.

Chapter 7. Your Next Step

"When I loved myself enough, I began leaving whatever wasn't healthy. This meant people, jobs, my own beliefs, and habits – anything that kept me small. My judgment called it disloyal. Now I see it as self-loving." - Kim Mcmillen

CONGRATULATIONS! You made it! Please spend time reflecting on these questions and answer them in your journal.

1. How do you feel about yourself compared to before you started this adventure? How would you rate the level of your self-love? Is there an improvement?

2. What do you think of yourself? Are there changes in your perception of yourself?

3. How do you treat yourself now when no one is watching or you experience failure?

4. You've been keeping a journal for the past few weeks. What has changed in your journal entries over time? Do you feel more in touch with yourself in your entries? Do your entries show you are more compassionate with yourself?

5. Are there any daily adventure activities that have become habits now? How do those habits improve your self-concept? What habit do you need to develop that will help make a significant shift in your life to get to your desired life?

6. What can you do going forward to improve your love for yourself further?

Be proud of yourself. Thirty days of learning to love and appreciate yourself is a fantastic achievement. Still, it's only a small step on a bigger journey.

Completely accepting and loving yourself is a process. You may encounter hiccups along the way. Sometimes, there are setbacks, hindrances, and difficulties, especially when facing your shadows, inner monsters, stress triggers, and emotional vampires, *but keep going*. Use those unpleasant circumstances as opportunities to know yourself more. Your increasing self-knowledge will take you to a deeper love for yourself.

You will love and enjoy your life more as you've learned that the values of your society don't determine your worth. You can set your own criteria. You can appreciate yourself and progress toward your vision of your best life. When you believe that you're becoming a better version of yourself each day, you will be pleased with yourself.

Begin thinking about how you can move forward from this new starting point. The tools and strategies you learn in your 30-day adventure to find your lost self are the beginning of the extraordinary future that awaits you!

Where will you go next?

Continue with the journey to increasing your love for yourself. When you need help, find an accountability partner to hold you accountable on this journey. You can hire me as your coach or enroll in our *Self-Love Mastery: Unlock and Love Your Authentic Self* program to help you deeply love yourself. There are also different resources you can find on the internet. Visit our website lovehealbelieve. com and sign up for our free resources.

God bless you, beautiful you! May you always live in the power of love!

Appendix

Personal Trigger Journal

How to Capture Triggers

1. Track the time you experience stress for at least 5 to 7 days. As much as possible, journal your experience while it is still fresh in your mind.
2. What were the events that led you to stress? Who were the people there? What did they say, did, or did not do that caused your stress?
3. Pay attention to how your body feels when your triggers appear. For example, what part of your body reacted first? Was it your head, shoulder, lower back, etc.?
4. What were your thoughts when it happened and how it affected your feelings?
5. What was your reaction or response as the event progressed? Did you leave the room angry, feel numb, etc.?
6. Do your reflection on your triggers
7. Plan on what you will do before, during, and after to prevent the triggers from showing up or lowering their influence on you.

DATE & TIME	EVENT	FEELINGS, THOUGHTS, BODY SENSATIONS THAT ARISE DUE TO THE EVENT	RESPONSE/REACTION (BEHAVIOR) I.E., CURSE, SLAM DOOR, WALK AWAY, ETC	CONSEQUENCES OF BEHAVIOR (SELF) I.E., GUILTY, FEEL GOOD, REGRET

Reflection

TOP 2 COMMON STRESS TRIGGERS	WHAT ARE YOUR THOUGHT PATTERN WHEN TRIGGERED?	WHAT ARE YOUR EMOTIONS AND FEELINGS PATTERN WHEN TRIGGERED?	WHAT PART OF YOUR BODY FEELS TIGHT OR TENSED?

Plan of Action

How to Respond Proactively with Triggers.

Now that you know your triggers and reactions, what changes are you going to take to control your response to triggers?

	Trigger 1	Trigger 2
Before How will you prevent the triggers from occurring? How will you stay away from triggers? How will you prepare yourself to control your response when triggers show up?		
During How can you proactively respond to triggers?		
After How will you show compassion to yourself if you give in to your triggers? How will you affirm yourself?		
What did you learn from your experience?		

Acknowledgement

Every time I share my story, I get a comment that I should write a book. But, more than ten years later, I still didn't dare to write until now. I am so grateful for those who help me take this step in writing my first book.

First, I want to thank God for giving me the courage and putting people on my way to help me overcome my inner struggles.

I am grateful to my family, especially my husband, Kimmo for loving and accepting me as I am. You are a gift of God to me. I am thankful for my parents, Coling and Inting. They are always there for me. My siblings, Jubilee Tampos, Efren Tampos, Marilyn Tampos Villadolid, and Julito Tampos, for their unconditional support. For my nephews and nieces, who make my heart sing. For my sisters-in-law, especially Kathy Mae Burgos, who is supporting my technology and social media fun stuff.

I'm forever thankful to Carol Costello and Michelle Hodges for editing this book and your friendship.

I am incredibly grateful for the Missionaries of the Assumption, for they were the ones who introduced me to a journey to my inner self. I am thankful for my formators, the leadership, my fellow formands, and all the M.A. sisters, for in you, I feel unconditional acceptance of my limitations. I know I am where I am now with your help. Thank you, Bebing, Nancy, Domelie, Anna, and Abel, for encouraging me and making the arduous journey to my inner self lighter. I will never forget our experience in the convent as juniors.

Thank you, Christ Youth in Action (CYA). When I felt so many insecurities in my younger years, you came into my life, and my CYA brothers and sisters made me feel I belonged.

I am grateful for the Redemptorist Community in the Philippines, especially to Fr. Will Quijano, my former spiritual director, who introduces me to the Missionaries of the Assumption and the Redemptorist Itinerant Mission Team. I came to know more about myself being part of the team.

I am grateful for the Life on Fire Family, especially our coaches, Nick Unsworth, Meghan Unsworth, and James Malinchak, for constantly inspiring me to live my God's given mission. I am so blessed to be part of this awesome and supportive Community. To Tony Robbins and Dean Graziosi, thank you for the Self-Education Revolution. I feel blessed to be part of your community.

Thank you, Suzanne Monroe, Founder of the International Association of Wellness Professionals (IAWP). Thank you for continually inspiring us and giving us resources and support to be better wellness coaches and the entire IAWP community.

To my co-workers and administrators at Madison Heights, especially the Developmental Preschool team and SPED administrators, and my former co-workers and administrators at Papago Elementary School, thank you for making my workplace fun and for your support.

Thank you to Pam Ross, PhD, Mary Zaragoza, and Laura Sanchez-Ramirez, for believing in me and for your prayers and encouragement.

For my students with disabilities, I love you, and I feel so blessed and honored that God has chosen me to serve you. One of my happiest moments is when I am in the classroom with you. Thank you.

I am grateful to you who bought, shared, and read this book. Part of the proceeds of this book will help fund the Hope Oasis Team to build a center for children with disabilities in the Philippines.

About the Author

Dolly Tampos Oksman, MA, MAED-SPED, is a Motivational Speaker, Special Education Teacher, Behavior Analyst, and a Certified Wellness Coach. She is the Founder and Owner of Love. Heal. Believe. LLC

Dolly is helping busy working women reduce their unhealthy stress and love themselves to live a happy, fulfilled life with an inner peace and calm that they love to wake up to each day.

Dolly received both her Bachelor's and Master's in Sociology from Mindanao State University-Iligan Institute of Technology in 1996 and 2004, respectively, earning the Academic Excellence Award and Best Thesis Award. In 1997 she taught Sociology and Anthropology as a Graduate Teaching Assistant for the Department of Sociology at MSU-IIT.

In 1999, Dolly volunteered with the Redemptorist Mission Team to gain exposure to Basic Ecclesial Communities. Dolly's missionary work continued from 2000 to 2005 as she joined Missionaries of the Assumption—a society of apostolic life. Throughout Dolly's missionary work, she advocated for women's empowerment, equal opportunity, justice and peace.

In 2007, Dolly moved to the United States. In 2012, Dolly received her Master's of Arts in Education with emphasis in Special Education from the University of Phoenix and in the same year, she started teaching children with disabilities.

Teaching special needs children gives her new meaning and purpose in life.

As a teacher, Dolly experiences how stress affects the well-being of many professionals working with children with disabilities. Having been able to hack the anatomy of her stress and her roller coaster emotions, she figured out the long-term solution to stress and how to quickly transform her emotional state.

As a result, Dolly became a wellness coach to help women live healthier lifestyles with less stress. In 2020, the International Association of Wellness Professionals certified her as a wellness coach.

Dolly Oksman lives in Arizona with her husband, Kimmo and niece, Bea.

To Learn more about Dolly, visit her website at lovehealbelieve.com.

References

American Psychological Association. (n.d.). *Apa PsycNet*. American Psychological Association. Retrieved December 4, 2022, from https://psycnet.apa.org/record/2020-29966-008

Carl Rogers and humanist psychotherapy. (2009). *Personality Theories: Critical Perspectives,* https://doi.org/10.4135/9781452231617.n12

Claretian Communications Foundation, Inc. (2010). The Catholic Prayer Bible: New revised standard version.

Dispenza, J., & Amen, D. G. (2015). *Breaking the habit of being yourself: How to lose your mind and create a new one.* Hay House.

Emoto, M., & Thayne, D. A. (2011). The secret *life of water*. Atria Paperback.

Erieau, C. (2022, March 20). 55 *best stress quotes - driven*. Driven Resilience. Retrieved December 4, 2022, from https://home.hellodriven.com/articles/55-best-stress-quotes/

Janse, B. (2022, March 9). *Four stages of competence*. Toolshero. Retrieved December 23, 2022, from https://www.toolshero.com/personal-development/four-stages-of-competence/

Kluger, J. (2015, June 26). *Consciousness: It's less than you think*. Time. Retrieved December 4, 2022, from https://time.com/3937351/consciousness-unconsciousness-brain

Lally, P., van Jaarsveld, C. H., Potts, H. W., & Wardle, J. (2009). How are habits formed: Modeling Habit Formation in the real world. *European Journal of Social Psychology,* 40(6), 998–1009. https://doi.org/10.1002/ejsp.674

Littlefield, C. (2021, October 11). *Do compliments make you cringe? here's why*. Harvard Business Review. Retrieved December 4, 2022, from https://hbr.org/2021/04/do-compliments-make-you-cringe-heres-why

Mayo Foundation for Medical Education and Research. (2022, November 15). *Narcissistic personality disorder*. Mayo Clinic. Retrieved December 4, 2022, from https://www.mayoclinic.org/diseases-conditions/narcissistic-personality-disorder/symptoms-causes/syc-20366662

Mastroianni, B. (2020, May 17). *Why Americans are more stressed today than they were in the 1990s*. Healthline. Retrieved December 4, 2022, from https://www.healthline.com/health-news/people-more-stressed-today-than-1990s

Merriam-Webster. (n.d.). Dictionary by *Merriam-Webster: America's most-trusted online dictionary*. Merriam-Webster. Retrieved December 23, 2022, from https://www.merriam-webster.com/

Robbins, M. (2017). *The 5 second rule: The fastest way to change your life*. Savio Republic.

Self-esteem. Encyclopedia of Children's Health. (n.d.). Retrieved December 4, 2022, from http://www.healthofchildren.com/S/Self-Esteem.html

Suni, E. (2022, August 29). *How much sleep do we really need?* Sleep Foundation. Retrieved December 23, 2022, from https://www.sleepfoundation.org/how-sleep-works/how-much-sleep-do-we-really-need

Weaver, J. (2006). *Having a Mary spirit: Allowing god to change us from the inside out*. WaterBrook Press.

8 Ways Priority Management Trumps Time Management. Lighthouse. (2022, October 18). Retrieved December 4, 2022, from https://getlighthouse.com/blog/why-priority-management-trumps-time-management/

Articles. 6 keys to learn anything faster BE FAST by Jim Kwik | Tuition Agency. (n.d.). Retrieved December 23, 2022, from https://acetutors.com.sg/6-keys-to-learn-anything-faster-BE-FAST-by-Jim-Kwik

www.ingramcontent.com/pod-product-compliance
Lightning Source LLC
Chambersburg PA
CBHW021637120626
46545CB00002B/582